DEPARTMENT OF THE TREASURY

Office of Foreign Assets Control

31 CFR Part 542

Syrian Sanctions Regulations

AGENCY: Office of Foreign Assets Control, Treasury.

ACTION: Final rule.

SUMMARY: The Department of the Treasury's Office of Foreign Assets Control ("OFAC") is amending the Syrian Sanctions Regulations (the "Regulations") and reissuing them in their entirety, in order to implement Executive Order 13399 of April 25, 2006, "Blocking Property of Additional Persons in Connection With the National Emergency With Respect to Syria," Executive Order 13460 of February 13, 2008, "Blocking Property of Additional Persons in Connection With the National Emergency With Respect to Syria," Executive Order 13572 of April 29, 2011, "Blocking Property of Certain Persons with Respect to Human Rights Abuses in Syria," Executive Order 13573 of May 18, 2011, "Blocking Property of Senior Officials of the Government of Syria," Executive Order 13582 of August 17, 2011, "Blocking Property of the Government of Syria and Prohibiting Certain Transactions with Respect to Syria," and Executive Order 13606 of April 22, 2012, "Blocking the Property and Suspending Entry Into the United States of Certain Persons with Respect to Grave Human Rights Abuses by the Governments of Iran and Syria via Information Technology." OFAC is also incorporating into the Regulations several new general licenses, some of which have, until now, appeared only on OFAC's Web site on the Syria sanctions page. Finally, OFAC is updating certain provisions of the Regulations and making other technical and conforming changes.

DATES: *Effective Date:* May 2, 2014.

FOR FURTHER INFORMATION CONTACT: Assistant Director for Sanctions Compliance & Evaluation, tel.: 202/622–2490, Assistant Director for Licensing, tel.: 202/622–2480, Assistant Director for Policy, tel.: 202/622–6746, Assistant Director for Regulatory Affairs, tel.: 202/622–4855, Office of Foreign Assets Control, or Chief Counsel (Foreign Assets Control), tel.: 202/622–2410, Office of the General Counsel, Department of the Treasury (not toll free numbers).

SUPPLEMENTARY INFORMATION:

Electronic and Facsimile Availability

This document and additional information concerning the Office of Foreign Assets Control (OFAC) are available from OFAC's Web site (*www.treasury.gov/ofac*). Certain general information pertaining to OFAC's sanctions programs also is available via facsimile through a 24-hour fax-on-demand service, tel.: 202/622–0077.

Background

On April 5, 2005, OFAC issued the Syrian Sanctions Regulations, 31 CFR part 542 (the "Regulations") (70 FR 17201, April 5, 2005), to implement Executive Order 13338 of May 11, 2004 (69 FR 26751, May 13, 2004) ("E.O. 13338"). OFAC today is amending the Regulations to implement Executive Order 13399 of April 25, 2006 (71 FR 25059, April 28, 2006) ("E.O. 13399"), Executive Order 13460 of February 13, 2008 (73 FR 8991, February 15, 2008) ("E.O. 13460"), Executive Order 13572 of April 29, 2011 (76 FR 24787, May 3, 2011) ("E.O. 13572"), Executive Order 13573 of May 18, 2011 (76 FR 29143, May 20, 2011) ("E.O. 13573"), Executive Order 13582 of August 17, 2011 (76 FR 52209, August 22, 2011) ("E.O. 13582"), and Executive Order 13606 of April 22, 2012 (77 FR 24571, April 24, 2012) ("E.O. 13606"). OFAC also is incorporating into the Regulations several new general licenses, some of which have, until now, appeared only on OFAC's Web site on the Syria sanctions page. Finally, OFAC is updating certain provisions of the Regulations and making other technical and conforming changes. Due to the extensive nature of these amendments, OFAC is reissuing the Regulations in their entirety.

On April 25, 2006, to take additional steps with respect to the national emergency with respect to Syria declared in E.O. 13338, the President issued E.O. 13399, invoking the authority of, *inter alia,* the International Emergency Economic Powers Act (50 U.S.C. 1701–1706) ("IEEPA"), the National Emergencies Act (50 U.S.C. 1601 *et seq.*) (the "NEA"), and section 5 of the United Nations Participation Act, as amended (22 U.S.C. 287c) ("UNPA"), and in view of United Nations Security Council Resolution ("UNSCR") 1636 of October 31, 2005. UNSCR 1636 requires member states to freeze the assets of individuals designated by the international independent investigation commission (the "Commission") established by UNSCR 1595 of April 7, 2005, or by the Government of Lebanon as suspected of involvement in the planning,

sponsoring, organizing, or perpetrating of the terrorist bombing in Beirut, Lebanon, on February 14, 2005, that killed former Lebanese Prime Minister Rafiq Hariri and 22 others.

Section 1(a) of E.O. 13399 blocks, with certain exceptions, all property and interests in property that are in the United States, that come within the United States, or that are or come within the possession or control of any United States person, including any overseas branch, of any person determined by the Secretary of the Treasury, after consultation with the Secretary of State: (1) To be, or to have been, involved in the planning, sponsoring, organizing, or perpetrating of (a) the terrorist act in Beirut, Lebanon, that resulted in the assassination of former Lebanese Prime Minister Rafiq Hariri and the deaths of 22 others; or (b) any other bombing, assassination, or assassination attempt in Lebanon since October 1, 2004, that is related to Hariri's assassination or that implicates the Government of Syria or its officers or agents; (2) to have obstructed or otherwise impeded the work of the Commission established pursuant to UNSCR 1595; (3) to have materially assisted, sponsored, or provided financial, material, or technological support for, or goods or services in support of, any such terrorist act, bombing, or assassination attempt, or any person designated pursuant to E.O. 13399; or (4) to be owned or controlled by, or acting or purporting to act for or on behalf of, directly or indirectly, any person designated pursuant to E.O. 13399. The property and interests in property of such persons may not be transferred, paid, exported, withdrawn, or otherwise dealt in.

The President issued E.O. 13460 on February 13, 2008, pursuant to the authority of, *inter alia,* IEEPA and the NEA, to take additional steps with respect to the national emergency declared in E.O. 13338. Section 1(a) of E.O. 13460 blocks, with certain exceptions, all property and interests in property that are in the United States, that come within the United States, or that are or come within the possession or control of any United States person, including any overseas branch, of any person determined by the Secretary of the Treasury, after consultation with the Secretary of State, to be responsible for, to have engaged in, to have facilitated, or to have secured improper advantage as a result of, public corruption by senior officials within the Government of Syria. The property and interests in property of such persons may not be transferred, paid, exported, withdrawn, or otherwise dealt in.

In addition, Section 2 of E.O. 13460 amends one of the criteria for designation pursuant to E.O. 13338 relating to undermining efforts to stabilize Iraq.

The President issued E.O. 13572 on April 29, 2011, pursuant to the authority of, *inter alia,* IEEPA and the NEA. In E.O. 13572, the President expanded the scope of the national emergency declared in E.O. 13338, finding that the Government of Syria's human rights abuses, including those related to the repression of the people of Syria, manifested most recently by the use of violence and torture against, and arbitrary arrests and detentions of, peaceful protestors by police, security forces, and other entities that have engaged in human rights abuses, constitute an unusual and extraordinary threat to the national security, foreign policy, and economy of the United States.

Section 1 of E.O. 13572 blocks all property and interests in property that are in the United States, that come within the United States, or that are or come within the possession or control of any United States person, including any overseas branch, of the persons listed in the Annex to E.O. 13572 and any person determined by the Secretary of the Treasury, in consultation with the Secretary of State: (1) To be responsible for or complicit in, or responsible for ordering, controlling, or otherwise directing, or to have participated in, the commission of human rights abuses in Syria, including those related to repression; (2) to be a senior official of an entity whose property and interests in property are blocked pursuant to E.O. 13572; (3) to have materially assisted, sponsored, or provided financial, material, or technological support for, or goods or services in support of, the activities described in (1) above or any person whose property and interests in property are blocked pursuant to E.O. 13338, E.O. 13460, or E.O. 13572; or (4) to be owned or controlled by, or to have acted or purported to act for or on behalf of, directly or indirectly, any person whose property and interests in property are blocked pursuant to E.O. 13460 or E.O. 13572. The property and interests in property of such persons may not be transferred, paid, exported, withdrawn, or otherwise dealt in.

The President issued E.O. 13573 on May 18, 2011, pursuant to the authority of, *inter alia,* IEEPA and the NEA, to take additional steps with respect to the national emergency declared in E.O. 13338 and expanded in scope in E.O. 13572.

Section 1 of E.O. 13573 blocks all property and interests in property that are in the United States, that come within the United States, or that are or come within the possession or control of any United States person, including any overseas branch, of the persons listed in the Annex to E.O. 13573 and any person determined by the Secretary of the Treasury, in consultation with the Secretary of State: (1) To be a senior official of the Government of Syria; (2) to be an agency or instrumentality of the Government of Syria, or owned or controlled, directly or indirectly, by the Government of Syria or by an official or officials of the Government of Syria; (3) to have materially assisted, sponsored, or provided financial, material, or technological support for, or goods or services in support of, any person whose property and interests in property are blocked pursuant to E.O. 13573; or (4) to be owned or controlled by, or to have acted or purported to act for or on behalf of, directly or indirectly, any person whose property and interests in property are blocked pursuant to E.O. 13573. The property and interests in property of such persons may not be transferred, paid, exported, withdrawn, or otherwise dealt in.

The President issued E.O. 13582 on August 17, 2011, pursuant to the authority of, *inter alia,* IEEPA and the NEA, to take additional steps with respect to the national emergency declared in E.O. 13338 and expanded in scope in E.O. 13572.

Section 1(a) of E.O. 13582 blocks all property and interests in property that are in the United States, that come within the United States, or that are or come within the possession or control of any United States person, including any overseas branch, of the Government of Syria. The term *Government of Syria* is defined in section 8(d) of E.O. 13582 to mean the Government of the Syrian Arab Republic, its agencies, instrumentalities, and controlled entities. The property and interests in property of the Government of Syria may not be transferred, paid, exported, withdrawn, or otherwise dealt in.

Section 1(b) of E.O. 13582 blocks all property and interests in property that are in the United States, that come within the United States, or that are or come within the possession or control of any United States person, including any overseas branch, of any person determined by the Secretary of the Treasury, in consultation with the Secretary of State: (1) To have materially assisted, sponsored, or provided financial, material, or technological support for, or goods or services in support of, any person whose property and interests in property are blocked pursuant to E.O. 13582; or (2) to be owned or controlled by, or to have acted or purported to act for or on behalf of, directly or indirectly, any person whose property and interests in property are blocked pursuant to E.O. 13582. The property and interests in property of such persons may not be transferred, paid, exported, withdrawn, or otherwise dealt in.

Section 2 of E.O. 13582 prohibits (1) new investment in Syria by a United States person, wherever located; (2) the exportation, reexportation, sale, or supply, directly or indirectly from the United States, or by a United States person, wherever located, of any services to Syria; (3) the importation into the United States of petroleum or petroleum products of Syrian origin; (4) any transaction or dealing by a United States person, wherever located, including purchasing, selling, transporting, swapping, brokering, approving, financing, facilitating, or guaranteeing, in or related to petroleum or petroleum products of Syrian origin; (5) any approval, financing, facilitation, or guarantee by a United States person, wherever located, of a transaction by a foreign person where the transaction by that foreign person would be prohibited by section 2 of E.O. 13582 if performed by a United States person or within the United States.

Section 7 of E.O. 13582 provides that nothing in sections 1 or 2 of the order shall prohibit transactions for the conduct of the official business of the Federal Government by employees, grantees, or contractors thereof.

The President issued E.O. 13606 on April 22, 2012, pursuant to the authority of, *inter alia,* IEEPA and the NEA, to take additional steps with respect to, *inter alia,* the national emergency declared in E.O. 13338 and expanded in scope in E.O. 13572.

Section 1 of E.O. 13606 blocks, in relevant part, all property and interests in property that are in the United States, that come within the United States, or that are or come within the possession or control of any United States person, including any foreign branch, of the persons listed in the Annex to E.O. 13606 and any person determined by the Secretary of the Treasury, in consultation with or at the recommendation of the Secretary of State: (1) To have operated, or to have directed the operation of, information and communications technology that facilitates computer or network disruption, monitoring, or tracking that could assist in or enable serious human rights abuses by or on behalf of the Government of Syria; (2) to have sold, leased, or otherwise provided, directly or indirectly, goods, services, or technology to Syria likely to be used to facilitate computer or network disruption, monitoring, or tracking that could assist in or enable serious human rights abuses by or on behalf of the Government of Syria; (3) to have materially assisted, sponsored, or provided financial, material, or technological support for, or goods or services to or in support of, the activities described in (1) or (2) above or any person whose property and interests in property are blocked pursuant to E.O. 13606; or (4) to be owned or controlled by, or to have acted or purported to act for or on behalf of, directly or indirectly, any person whose property and interests in property are blocked pursuant to E.O. 13606. The property and interests in property of such persons may not be transferred, paid, exported, withdrawn, or otherwise dealt in.

Section 6 of E.O. 13606 provides that nothing in section 1 of the order shall prohibit transactions for the conduct of the official business of the United States Government by employees, contractors, or grantees thereof.

In section 1(b) of E.O. 13399, section 5 of E.O. 13460, section 2 of E.O.s 13572, 13573, and 13606, and section 3 of E.O. 13582, the President determined that the making of donations of certain articles, such as food, clothing, and medicine, intended to be used to relieve human suffering, as specified in section 203(b)(2) of IEEPA (50 U.S.C. 1702(b)(2)), by, to, or for the benefit of any person whose property and interests in property are blocked pursuant to those orders would seriously impair his ability to deal with the national emergency declared in E.O. 13338. The President therefore prohibited such donations as provided by the orders.

Section 1(c) of E.O. 13399, section 1(b) of E.O. 13460, section 3 of E.O.s 13572, 13573, and 13606, and section 4 of E.O. 13582 provide that the prohibition on any transaction or dealing in blocked property or interests in property includes, but is not limited to, the making of any contribution or provision of funds, goods, or services by, to, or for the benefit of any person whose property and interests in property are blocked pursuant to those orders, and the receipt of any contribution or provision of funds, goods, or services from any such person.

Section 5 of E.O. 13399, section 7 of E.O. 13460, section 8 of E.O.s 13572 and 13573, section 9 of E.O. 13606, and section 10 of E.O. 13582 authorize the Secretary of the Treasury, in consultation with the Secretary of State, to take such actions, including the promulgation of rules and regulations, and to employ all powers granted to the President by IEEPA as may be necessary to carry out the purposes of those orders. These sections also authorize the Secretary of the Treasury to redelegate any of these functions to other officers and agencies of the U.S. Government consistent with applicable law.

Subpart A of the Regulations clarifies the relation of this part to other laws and regulations. Subpart B of the Regulations sets forth the prohibitions contained in the various Executive orders. Accordingly, section 542.201 in subpart B has been expanded to include the blocking prohibitions in E.O.s 13399, 13460, 13572, 13573, 13582, and 13606. New sections 542.206 through 542.210 are being added to subpart B to set forth additional prohibitions imposed in section 2 of E.O. 13582. In subpart C, which defines key terms used throughout the Regulations, new sections 542.304 through 542.306, 542.310, 542.311, 542.312, 542.314, 542.316, 542.320, 542.322, and 542.323 are being added to define key terms used in the new blocking prohibitions or elsewhere in the Regulations. Because these new definitions were inserted in alphabetical order, certain previously existing definitions have been renumbered. In subpart D, which contains interpretive sections regarding the Regulations, new sections 542.411 through 542.413 are being added, and former section 542.405 is being expanded.

Transactions otherwise prohibited under the Regulations but found to be consistent with U.S. policy may be authorized by one of the general licenses contained in subpart E of the Regulations or by a specific license issued pursuant to the procedures described in subpart E of 31 CFR part 501. Subpart E of the Regulations also contains certain statements of licensing policy in addition to the general licenses. New general licenses that previously had been posted only on OFAC's Web site are being added in sections 542.509 through 542.520 and 542.523. In addition, sections 542.508, 542.521, 542.522, 542.524, 542.525, and 542.526 incorporate new general licenses and sections 542.527, 542.528, and 542.529 incorporate new statements of licensing policy. Revisions also are being made to the authorizations in section 542.507.

In addition to the authorizations in Subpart E, on September 9, 2011, OFAC issued a general license on its Web site (Syria General License No. 7), which authorized the wind down of contracts involving the Government of Syria and the divestiture of a U.S. person's investments or winding down of contracts involving Syria. This general license expired on November 26, 2011.

Additionally, the general license formerly found at section 542.508, which authorizes the provision of nonscheduled emergency medical services in the United States to persons whose property or interests in property are blocked pursuant to section 542.201(a), can now be found at section 542.531.

Subpart F of the Regulations refers to subpart C of part 501 for recordkeeping and reporting requirements. Subpart G of the Regulations describes the civil and criminal penalties applicable to violations of the Regulations, as well as the procedures governing the potential imposition of a civil monetary penalty.

Subpart H of the Regulations refers to subpart E of part 501 for applicable provisions relating to administrative procedures and contains a delegation of authority by the Secretary of the Treasury. Subpart I of the Regulations sets forth a Paperwork Reduction Act notice.

Public Participation

Because the Regulations involve a foreign affairs function, the provisions of Executive Order 12866 and the Administrative Procedure Act (5 U.S.C. 553) requiring notice of proposed rulemaking, opportunity for public participation, and delay in effective date are inapplicable. Because no notice of proposed rulemaking is required for this rule, the Regulatory Flexibility Act (5 U.S.C. 601–612) does not apply.

Paperwork Reduction Act

The collections of information related to the Regulations are contained in 31 CFR part 501 (the "Reporting, Procedures and Penalties Regulations"). Pursuant to the Paperwork Reduction Act of 1995 (44 U.S.C. 3507), those collections of information have been approved by the Office of Management and Budget under control number 1505–0164. An agency may not conduct or sponsor, and a person is not required to respond to, a collection of information unless the collection of information displays a valid control number.

List of Subjects in 31 CFR Part 542

Administrative practice and procedure, Banks, Banking, Blocking of assets, Credit, Investments, Penalties, Reporting and recordkeeping requirements, Securities, Services, Syria.

For the reasons set forth in the preamble, the Department of the Treasury's Office of Foreign Assets Control amends 31 CFR chapter V by revising 31 CFR part 542 to read as follows:

PART 542—SYRIAN SANCTIONS REGULATIONS

Authority: 3 U.S.C. 301; 31 U.S.C. 321(b); 18 U.S.C. 2332d; 22 U.S.C. 287c; 50 U.S.C. 1601–1651, 1701–1706; Pub. L. 101–410, 104 Stat. 890 (28 U.S.C. 2461 note); Pub. L. 110–96, 121 Stat. 1011 (50 U.S.C. 1701 note); E.O. 13338, 69 FR 26751, 3 CFR, 2004 Comp., p. 168; E.O. 13399, 71 FR 25059, 3 CFR, 2006 Comp., p. 218; E.O. 13460, 73 FR 8991, 3 CFR 2008 Comp., p. 181; E.O. 13572, 76 FR 24787, 3 CFR 2011 Comp., p. 236; E.O. 13573, 76 FR 29143, 3 CFR 2011 Comp., p. 241; E.O. 13582, 76 FR 52209, 3 CFR 2011 Comp., p. 264; E.O. 13606, 77 FR 24571, 3 CFR 2012 Comp., p. 243.

Subpart A—Relation of This Part to Other Laws and Regulations

§ 542.101 Relation of this part to other laws and regulations.

This part is separate from, and independent of, the other parts of this chapter, with the exception of part 501 of this chapter, the recordkeeping and reporting requirements and license application and other procedures of which apply to this part. Actions taken pursuant to part 501 of this chapter with respect to the prohibitions contained in this part are considered actions taken pursuant to this part. Differing foreign policy and national security circumstances may result in differing interpretations of similar language among the parts of this chapter. No license or authorization contained in or issued pursuant to those other parts authorizes any transaction prohibited by this part. No license or authorization contained in or issued pursuant to any other provision of law or regulation authorizes any transaction prohibited by this part. No license or authorization contained in or issued pursuant to this part relieves the involved parties from complying with any other applicable laws or regulations.

Subpart B—Prohibitions

§ 542.201 Prohibited transactions involving blocked property.

(a)(1) All property and interests in property that are in the United States, that come within the United States, or that are or come within the possession or control of any United States person, including any foreign branch, of the Government of Syria and of the following persons are blocked and may not be transferred, paid, exported, withdrawn, or otherwise dealt in: Any person determined by the Secretary of the Treasury, in consultation with the Secretary of State:

(i) To have materially assisted, sponsored, or provided financial, material, or technological support for, or goods or services in support of, the Government of Syria or any other person whose property and interests in property are blocked pursuant to paragraph (a)(1) of this section; or

(ii) To be owned or controlled by, or to have acted or purported to act for or on behalf of, directly or indirectly, the Government of Syria or any other person whose property and interests in property are blocked pursuant to paragraph (a)(1) of this section.

(2) All property and interests in property that are in the United States, that come within the United States, or that are or come within the possession or control of any United States person, including any foreign branch, of the following persons are blocked and may not be transferred, paid, exported, withdrawn, or otherwise dealt in:

(i) The persons listed in the Annex to Executive Order 13572 of April 29, 2011, and the Annex to Executive Order 13573 of May 18, 2011; and

(ii) Any person determined by the Secretary of the Treasury, in consultation with the Secretary of State:

(A) To be or to have been directing or otherwise significantly contributing to the Government of Syria's provision of safe haven to or other support for any person whose property and interests in property are blocked under United States law for terrorism-related reasons, including, but not limited to, Hamas, Hizballah, Palestinian Islamic Jihad, the Popular Front for the Liberation of Palestine, the Popular Front for the Liberation of Palestine-General Command, and any persons designated pursuant to Executive Order 13224 of September 23, 2001;

(B) To be or to have been directing or otherwise significantly contributing to the Government of Syria's military or security presence in Lebanon;

(C) To be or to have been directing or otherwise significantly contributing to the Government of Syria's pursuit of the development and production of chemical, biological, or nuclear weapons and medium- and long-range surface-to-surface missiles;

(D) To be or to have been responsible for or otherwise significantly contributing to actions taken or decisions made by the Government of Syria that have the purpose or effect of undermining efforts to stabilize Iraq or of allowing the use of Syrian territory or facilities to undermine efforts to stabilize Iraq;

(E) To be or to have been involved in the planning, sponsoring, organizing, or perpetrating of:

(*1*) The terrorist act in Beirut, Lebanon, that resulted in the assassination of former Lebanese Prime Minister Rafiq Hariri and the deaths of 22 others; or

(*2*) Any other bombing, assassination, or assassination attempt in Lebanon since October 1, 2004, that is related to Hariri's assassination or that implicates the Government of Syria or its officers or agents;

(F) To have obstructed or otherwise impeded the work of the Commission established pursuant to United Nations Security Council Resolution 1595 of April 7, 2005;

(G) To be responsible for, to have engaged in, to have facilitated, or to have secured improper advantage as a result of, public corruption by senior officials within the Government of Syria;

(H) To be responsible for or complicit in, or responsible for ordering, controlling, or otherwise directing, or to have participated in, the commission of human rights abuses in Syria, including those related to repression;

(I) To be a senior official of an entity whose property and interests in property are blocked pursuant to paragraph (a)(2)(ii)(H) of this section or any other entity whose property and interests in property are blocked pursuant to E.O. 13572;

(J) To be a senior official of the Government of Syria;

(K) To be an agency or instrumentality of the Government of Syria, or owned or controlled, directly or indirectly, by the Government of Syria or by an official or officials of the Government of Syria;

(L) To have materially assisted, sponsored, or provided financial, material, or technological support for, or goods or services in support of, the activities described in paragraph (a)(2)(ii)(E) or (H) of this section, or any person whose property and interests in property are blocked pursuant to paragraph (a)(2) of this section; or

(M) To be owned or controlled by, or to have acted or purported to act for or on behalf of, directly or indirectly, any person whose property and interests in property are blocked pursuant to paragraph (a)(2) of this section.

(3) All property and interests in property that are in the United States, that come within the United States, or that are or come within the possession or control of any United States person, including any foreign branch, of the following persons are blocked and may not be transferred, paid, exported, withdrawn, or otherwise dealt in:

(i) The persons listed in the Annex to Executive Order 13606 of April 22, 2012; and

(ii) Any person determined by the Secretary of the Treasury, in consultation with or at the recommendation of the Secretary of State:

(A) To have operated, or to have directed the operation of, information and communications technology that facilitates computer or network disruption, monitoring, or tracking that could assist in or enable serious human rights abuses by or on behalf of the Government of Syria;

(B) To have sold, leased, or otherwise provided, directly or indirectly, goods, services, or technology to Syria likely to be used to facilitate computer or network disruption, monitoring, or tracking that could assist in or enable serious human rights abuses by or on behalf of the Government of Syria;

(C) To have materially assisted, sponsored, or provided financial, material, or technological support for, or goods or services in support of, the activities described in paragraph (a)(3)(ii)(A) or (B) of this section, or any person whose property and interests in property are blocked pursuant to paragraph (a)(3) of this section; or

(D) To be owned or controlled by, or to have acted or purported to act for or on behalf of, directly or indirectly, any person whose property and interests in property are blocked pursuant to paragraph (a)(3) of this section.

Note 1 to paragraph (a) of § 542.201: The names of persons listed in or designated pursuant to Executive Order 13338 of May 11, 2004, Executive Order 13399 of April 25,

2006, Executive Order 13460 of February 13, 2008, Executive Order 13572 of April 29, 2011, Executive Order 13573 of May 18, 2011, Executive Order 13582 of August 17, 2011, or identified pursuant to E.O. 13582, whose property and interests in property are blocked pursuant to paragraph (a)(1) or (2) of this section, are published in the **Federal Register** and incorporated into OFAC's Specially Designated Nationals and Blocked Persons List ("SDN List") with the identifier "[SYRIA]." The names of persons listed in or designated pursuant to Executive Order 13606 of April 22, 2012, whose property and interests in property therefore are blocked pursuant to paragraph (a)(3) of this section, are published in the **Federal Register** and incorporated into the SDN List with the identifier "[HRIT–SY]." The SDN List is accessible through the following page on OFAC's Web site: *www.treasury.gov/sdn*. Additional information pertaining to the SDN List can be found in Appendix A to this chapter. *See* § 542.411 concerning entities that may not be listed on the SDN List but whose property and interests in property are nevertheless blocked pursuant to paragraph (a) of this section. Executive Order 13582 blocks the property and interests in property of the Government of Syria, as defined in § 542.305. The property and interests in property of persons falling within the definition of the term *Government of Syria* are blocked pursuant to paragraph (a) of this section regardless of whether the names of such persons are published in the **Federal Register** or incorporated into the SDN List.

Note 2 to paragraph (a) of § 542.201: The International Emergency Economic Powers Act (50 U.S.C. 1701–1706), in section 203 (50 U.S.C. 1702), authorizes the blocking of property and interests in property of a person during the pendency of an investigation. The names of persons whose property and interests in property are blocked pending investigation pursuant to paragraph (a) of this section also are published in the **Federal Register** and incorporated into the SDN List with the identifier "[BPI–SYRIA]" or "[BPI–HRIT–SY]," as applicable.

Note 3 to paragraph (a) of § 542.201: Sections 501.806 and 501.807 of this chapter describe the procedures to be followed by persons seeking, respectively, the unblocking of funds that they believe were blocked due to mistaken identity, or administrative reconsideration of their status as the Government of Syria or any other person whose property and interests in property are blocked pursuant to paragraph (a) of this section.

(b) The prohibitions in paragraph (a) of this section include, but are not limited to, prohibitions on the following transactions:

(1) The making of any contribution or provision of funds, goods, or services by, to, or for the benefit of any person whose property and interests in property are blocked pursuant to paragraph (a) of this section; and

(2) The receipt of any contribution or provision of funds, goods, or services from any person whose property and interests in property are blocked pursuant to paragraph (a) of this section.

(c) Unless authorized by this part or by a specific license expressly referring to this section, any dealing in any security (or evidence thereof) held within the possession or control of a U.S. person and either registered or inscribed in the name of, or known to be held for the benefit of, or issued by, the Government of Syria or any other person whose property and interests in property are blocked pursuant to paragraph (a) of this section is prohibited. This prohibition includes but is not limited to the transfer (including the transfer on the books of any issuer or agent thereof), disposition, transportation, importation, exportation, or withdrawal of, or the endorsement or guaranty of signatures on, any such security on or after the effective date. This prohibition applies irrespective of the fact that at any time (whether prior to, on, or subsequent to the effective date) the registered or inscribed owner of any such security may have or might appear to have assigned, transferred, or otherwise disposed of the security.

(d) The prohibitions in paragraph (a) of this section apply except to the extent transactions are authorized by regulations, orders, directives, rulings, instructions, licenses, or otherwise, and notwithstanding any contracts entered into or any license or permit granted prior to the effective date.

§ 542.202 Effect of transfers violating the provisions of this part.

(a) Any transfer after the effective date that is in violation of any provision of this part or of any regulation, order, directive, ruling, instruction, or license issued pursuant to this part, and that involves any property or interest in property blocked pursuant to § 542.201(a), is null and void and shall not be the basis for the assertion or recognition of any interest in or right, remedy, power, or privilege with respect to such property or property interest.

(b) No transfer before the effective date shall be the basis for the assertion or recognition of any right, remedy, power, or privilege with respect to, or any interest in, any property or interest in property blocked pursuant to § 542.201(a), unless the person who holds or maintains such property, prior to that date, had written notice of the transfer or by any written evidence had recognized such transfer.

(c) Unless otherwise provided, a license or other authorization issued by OFAC before, during, or after a transfer shall validate such transfer or make it enforceable to the same extent that it would be valid or enforceable but for the provisions of this part and any regulation, order, directive, ruling, instruction, or license issued pursuant to this part.

(d) Transfers of property that otherwise would be null and void or unenforceable by virtue of the provisions of this section shall not be deemed to be null and void or unenforceable as to any person with whom such property is or was held or maintained (and as to such person only) in cases in which such person is able to establish to the satisfaction of OFAC each of the following:

(1) Such transfer did not represent a willful violation of the provisions of this part by the person with whom such property is or was held or maintained (and as to such person only);

(2) The person with whom such property is or was held or maintained did not have reasonable cause to know or suspect, in view of all the facts and circumstances known or available to such person, that such transfer required a license or authorization issued pursuant to this part and was not so licensed or authorized, or, if a license or authorization did purport to cover the transfer, that such license or authorization had been obtained by misrepresentation of a third party or withholding of material facts or was otherwise fraudulently obtained; and

(3) The person with whom such property is or was held or maintained filed with OFAC a report setting forth in full the circumstances relating to such transfer promptly upon discovery that:

(i) Such transfer was in violation of the provisions of this part or any regulation, ruling, instruction, license, or other directive or authorization issued pursuant to this part;

(ii) Such transfer was not licensed or authorized by OFAC; or

(iii) If a license did purport to cover the transfer, such license had been obtained by misrepresentation of a third party or withholding of material facts or was otherwise fraudulently obtained.

Note to paragraph (d) of § 542.202: The filing of a report in accordance with the provisions of paragraph (d)(3) of this section shall not be deemed evidence that the terms of paragraphs (d)(1) and (2) of this section have been satisfied.

(e) Unless licensed pursuant to this part, any attachment, judgment, decree, lien, execution, garnishment, or other judicial process is null and void with respect to any property and interests in property blocked pursuant to § 542.201(a).

§ 542.203 Holding of funds in interest-bearing accounts; investment and reinvestment.

(a) Except as provided in paragraphs (e) or (f) of this section, or as otherwise directed by OFAC, any U.S. person holding funds, such as currency, bank deposits, or liquidated financial obligations, subject to § 542.201(a) shall hold or place such funds in a blocked interest-bearing account located in the United States.

(b)(1) For purposes of this section, the term *blocked interest-bearing account* means a blocked account:

(i) In a federally-insured U.S. bank, thrift institution, or credit union, provided the funds are earning interest at rates that are commercially reasonable; or

(ii) With a broker or dealer registered with the Securities and Exchange Commission under the Securities Exchange Act of 1934 (15 U.S.C. 78a *et seq.*), provided the funds are invested in a money market fund or in U.S. Treasury bills.

(2) Funds held or placed in a blocked account pursuant to paragraph (a) of this section may not be invested in instruments the maturity of which exceeds 180 days.

(c) For purposes of this section, a rate is commercially reasonable if it is the rate currently offered to other depositors on deposits or instruments of comparable size and maturity.

(d) For purposes of this section, if interest is credited to a separate blocked account or subaccount, the name of the account party on each account must be the same.

(e) Blocked funds held in instruments the maturity of which exceeds 180 days at the time the funds become subject to § 542.201(a) may continue to be held until maturity in the original instrument, provided any interest, earnings, or other proceeds derived therefrom are paid into a blocked interest-bearing account in accordance with paragraphs (a) or (f) of this section.

(f) Blocked funds held in accounts or instruments outside the United States at the time the funds become subject to § 542.201(a) may continue to be held in the same type of accounts or instruments, provided the funds earn interest at rates that are commercially reasonable.

(g) This section does not create an affirmative obligation for the holder of blocked tangible property, such as chattels or real estate, or of other blocked property, such as debt or equity securities, to sell or liquidate such property. However, OFAC may issue licenses permitting or directing such sales or liquidation in appropriate cases.

(h) Funds subject to this section may not be held, invested, or reinvested in a manner that provides immediate financial or economic benefit or access to any person whose property and interests in property are blocked pursuant to § 542.201(a), nor may their holder cooperate in or facilitate the pledging or other attempted use as collateral of blocked funds or other assets.

§ 542.204 Expenses of maintaining blocked physical property; liquidation of blocked property.

(a) Except as otherwise authorized, and notwithstanding the existence of any rights or obligations conferred or imposed by any international agreement or contract entered into or any license or permit granted prior to the effective date, all expenses incident to the maintenance of physical property blocked pursuant to § 542.201(a) shall be the responsibility of the owners or operators of such property, which expenses shall not be met from blocked funds.

(b) Property blocked pursuant to § 542.201(a) may, in the discretion of OFAC, be sold or liquidated and the net proceeds placed in a blocked interest-bearing account in the name of the owner of the property.

§ 542.205 Evasions; attempts; causing violations; conspiracies.

(a) Any transaction by a U.S. person or within the United States that evades or avoids, has the purpose of evading or avoiding, causes a violation of, or attempts to violate any of the prohibitions set forth in this part is prohibited.

(b) Any conspiracy formed to violate any of the prohibitions set forth in this part is prohibited.

§ 542.206 Prohibited new investment in Syria.

Except as otherwise authorized, new investment, as defined in § 542.311, in Syria by a United States person, wherever located, is prohibited.

§ 542.207 Prohibited exportation, reexportation, sale, or supply of services to Syria.

Except as otherwise authorized, the exportation, reexportation, sale, or supply, directly or indirectly, from the United States, or by a United States person, wherever located, of any services to Syria is prohibited.

§ 542.208 Prohibited importation of petroleum or petroleum products of Syrian origin.

Except as otherwise authorized, the importation into the United States of petroleum or petroleum products of Syrian origin is prohibited.

§ 542.209 Prohibited transactions or dealings in or related to petroleum or petroleum products of Syrian origin.

Except as otherwise authorized, any transaction or dealing by a United States person, wherever located, including purchasing, selling, transporting, swapping, brokering, approving, financing, facilitating, or guaranteeing, in or related to petroleum or petroleum products of Syrian origin is prohibited.

§ 542.210 Prohibited facilitation.

Except as otherwise authorized, United States persons, wherever located, are prohibited from approving, financing, facilitating, or guaranteeing a transaction by a foreign person where the transaction by that foreign person would be prohibited by §§ 542.206, 542.207, 542.208, or 542.209 of this part if performed by a United States person or within the United States.

§ 542.211 Exempt transactions.

(a) *Personal communications.* Except as set forth in paragraph (e) of this section, the prohibitions contained in this part do not apply to any postal, telegraphic, telephonic, or other personal communication that does not involve the transfer of anything of value.

(b) *Information or informational materials.* (1) Except as set forth in paragraph (e) of this section, the prohibitions contained in this part do not apply to the importation from any country and the exportation to any country of any information or informational materials, as defined in § 542.307, whether commercial or otherwise, regardless of format or medium of transmission.

(2) This section does not exempt from regulation or authorize transactions related to information or informational materials not fully created and in existence at the date of the transactions, or to the substantive or artistic alteration or enhancement of informational materials, or to the provision of marketing and business consulting services. Such prohibited transactions include, but are not limited to, payment of advances for information or informational materials not yet created and completed (with the exception of prepaid subscriptions for widely circulated magazines and other periodical publications); provision of services to market, produce or co-produce, create, or assist in the creation of information or informational materials; and payment of royalties with respect to income received for enhancements or alterations made by

U.S. persons to such information or informational materials.

(3) This section does not exempt or authorize transactions incident to the exportation of software subject to the Export Administration Regulations, 15 CFR parts 730 through 774, or to the exportation of goods (including software) or technology for use in the transmission of any data, or to the provision, sale, or leasing of capacity on telecommunications transmission facilities (such as satellite or terrestrial network connectivity) for use in the transmission of any data. The exportation of such items or services and the provision, sale, or leasing of such capacity or facilities to Syria or to the Government of Syria or any other person whose property and interests in property are blocked pursuant to § 542.201(a) are prohibited.

Note 1 to paragraph (b)(3) of § 542.211: *See* § 542.510 for a general license authorizing the exportation or reexportation of certain items and services to Syria.

Note 2 to paragraph (b)(3) of § 542.211: *See* § 542.511 for a general license authorizing the exportation to persons in Syria of certain services incident to the exchange of personal communications over the Internet.

(c) *Travel.* Except as set forth in paragraph (e) of this section, the prohibitions contained in this part do not apply to transactions ordinarily incident to travel to or from any country, including importation or exportation of accompanied baggage for personal use, maintenance within any country including payment of living expenses and acquisition of goods or services for personal use, and arrangement or facilitation of such travel including nonscheduled air, sea, or land voyages.

(d) *Official business.* The prohibitions contained in this part, other than those in § 542.201(a)(2), do not apply to transactions for the conduct of the official business of the Federal Government by employees, grantees, or contractors thereof.

Note to paragraph (d) of § 542.211: *See* § 542.522 for a general license authorizing transactions for the conduct of the official business of the Federal Government prohibited by § 542.201(a)(2).

(e) The exemptions described in this section do not apply to any transactions involving property or interests in property of certain persons whose property and interests in property are blocked pursuant to E.O. 13399.

Note to paragraph (e) of § 542.211: As of the date of publication in the **Federal Register**, no persons have been designated by OFAC pursuant to E.O. 13399.

Subpart C—General Definitions

§ 542.300 Applicability of definitions.

The definitions in this subpart apply throughout the entire part.

§ 542.301 Blocked account; blocked property.

The terms *blocked account* and *blocked property* shall mean any account or property subject to the prohibitions in § 542.201 held in the name of the Government of Syria or any other person whose property and interests in property are blocked pursuant to § 542.201(a), or in which such person has an interest, and with respect to which payments, transfers, exportations, withdrawals, or other dealings may not be made or effected except pursuant to an authorization or license from OFAC expressly authorizing such action.

Note to § 542.301: *See* § 542.411 concerning the blocked status of property and interests in property of an entity that is 50 percent or more owned by a person whose property and interests in property are blocked pursuant to § 542.201(a).

§ 542.302 Effective date.

The term *effective date* refers to the effective date of the applicable prohibitions and directives contained in this part as follows:

(a) With respect to prohibited transfers or other dealings in blocked property and interests in property of the Government of Syria, as defined in § 542.305, 12:01 a.m. eastern daylight time, August 18, 2011;

(b) With respect to a person whose property and interests in property are blocked pursuant to § 542.201(a)(2)(i), 1:00 p.m. eastern daylight time, April 29, 2011, for persons listed in the Annex to Executive Order 13572 of April 29, 2011, and 1:00 p.m. eastern daylight time, May 18, 2011, for persons listed in the Annex to Executive Order 13573 of May 18, 2011;

(c) With respect to a person whose property and interests in property are blocked pursuant to § 542.201(a)(3)(i), 12:01 a.m. eastern daylight time, April 23, 2012;

(d) With respect to a person whose property and interests in property are otherwise blocked pursuant to § 542.201(a), the earlier of the date of actual or constructive notice that such person's property and interests in property are blocked; and

(e) With respect to the prohibitions set forth in §§ 542.206 through 542.210, 12:01 a.m. eastern daylight time, August 18, 2011.

§ 542.303 Entity.

The term *entity* means a partnership, association, trust, joint venture, corporation, group, subgroup, or other organization.

§ 542.304 Financial, material, or technological support.

The term *financial, material, or technological support,* as used in § 542.201(a)(1)(i), (a)(2)(ii)(L), and (a)(3)(ii)(C), means any property, tangible or intangible, including but not limited to currency, financial instruments, securities, or any other transmission of value; weapons or related materiel; chemical or biological agents; explosives; false documentation or identification; communications equipment; computers; electronic or other devices or equipment; technologies; lodging; safe houses; facilities; vehicles or other means of transportation; or goods. "Technologies" as used in this definition means specific information necessary for the development, production, or use of a product, including related technical data such as blueprints, plans, diagrams, models, formulae, tables, engineering designs and specifications, manuals, or other recorded instructions.

§ 542.305 Government of Syria.

The term *Government of Syria* includes:

(a) The state and the Government of the Syrian Arab Republic, as well as any political subdivision, agency, or instrumentality thereof, including the Central Bank of Syria;

(b) Any entity owned or controlled, directly or indirectly, by the foregoing, including any corporation, partnership, association, or other entity in which the Government of Syria owns a 50 percent or greater interest or a controlling interest, and any entity which is otherwise controlled by that government;

(c) Any person that is, or has been, acting or purporting to act, directly or indirectly, for or on behalf of any of the foregoing; and

(d) Any other person determined by OFAC to be included within paragraphs (a) through (c) of this section.

Note 1 to § 542.305: The names of persons that OFAC has determined fall within this definition are published in the **Federal Register** and incorporated into OFAC's Specially Designated Nationals and Blocked Persons List ("SDN List") with the identifier "[SYRIA]." The SDN List is accessible through the following page on OFAC's Web site: *www.treasury.gov/sdn.* However, the property and interests in property of persons falling within the definition of the term *Government of Syria* are blocked pursuant to

§ 542.201(a) regardless of whether the names of such persons are published in the **Federal Register** or incorporated into the SDN List.

Note 2 to § 542.305: Section 501.807 of this chapter describes the procedures to be followed by persons seeking administrative reconsideration of OFAC's determination that they fall within the definition of the term *Government of Syria.*

§ 542.306 Information and communications technology.

The term *information and communications technology* means any hardware, software, or other product or service primarily intended to fulfill or enable the function of information processing and communication by electronic means, including transmission and display, including via the Internet.

§ 542.307 Information or informational materials.

(a) The term *information or informational materials* includes, but is not limited to, publications, films, posters, phonograph records, photographs, microfilms, microfiche, tapes, compact disks, CD ROMs, artworks, and news wire feeds.

Note to paragraph (a) of § 542.307: To be considered *information or informational materials,* artworks must be classified under chapter subheading 9701, 9702, or 9703 of the Harmonized Tariff Schedule of the United States.

(b) The term *information or informational materials,* with respect to exports, does not include items:
(1) That were, as of April 30, 1994, or that thereafter become, controlled for export pursuant to section 5 of the Export Administration Act of 1979, 50 U.S.C. App. 2401–2420 (1979) (the "EAA"), or section 6 of the EAA to the extent that such controls promote the nonproliferation or antiterrorism policies of the United States; or
(2) With respect to which acts are prohibited by 18 U.S.C. chapter 37.

§ 542.308 Interest.

Except as otherwise provided in this part, the term *interest,* when used with respect to property (*e.g.,* "an interest in property"), means an interest of any nature whatsoever, direct or indirect.

§ 542.309 Licenses; general and specific.

(a) Except as otherwise provided in this part, the term *license* means any license or authorization contained in or issued pursuant to this part.
(b) The term *general license* means any license or authorization the terms of which are set forth in subpart E of this part or made available on OFAC's Web site: *www.treasury.gov/ofac.*

(c) The term *specific license* means any license or authorization issued pursuant to this part, but not set forth in subpart E of this part or made available on OFAC's Web site: *www.treasury.gov/ofac.*

Note to § 542.309: *See* § 501.801 of this chapter on licensing procedures.

§ 542.310 Loans or other extensions of credit.

The term *loans or other extensions of credit* means any transfer or extension of funds or credit on the basis of an obligation to repay, or any assumption or guarantee of the obligation of another to repay an extension of funds or credit, including but not limited to: Overdrafts; currency swaps; purchases of debt securities issued by the Government of Syria; purchases of a loan made by another person; sales of financial assets subject to an agreement to repurchase; renewals or refinancings whereby funds or credits are transferred to or extended to a prohibited borrower or prohibited recipient; the issuance of standby letters of credit; and drawdowns on existing lines of credit.

§ 542.311 New investment.

The term *new investment* means a transaction after 12:01 a.m. eastern daylight time, August 18, 2011, that constitutes:
(a) A commitment or contribution of funds or other assets; or
(b) A loan or other extension of credit as defined in § 542.310.

§ 542.312 OFAC.

The term *OFAC* means the Department of the Treasury's Office of Foreign Assets Control.

§ 542.313 Person.

The term *person* means an individual or entity.

§ 542.314 Petroleum or petroleum products of Syrian origin.

The term *petroleum or petroleum products of Syrian origin* means petroleum or petroleum products of Syrian origin pursuant to Country of Origin definitions of U.S. Customs and Border Protection.

§ 542.315 Property; property interest.

The terms *property* and *property interest* include, but are not limited to, money, checks, drafts, bullion, bank deposits, savings accounts, debts, indebtedness, obligations, notes, guarantees, debentures, stocks, bonds, coupons, any other financial instruments, bankers acceptances, mortgages, pledges, liens or other rights in the nature of security, warehouse

receipts, bills of lading, trust receipts, bills of sale, any other evidences of title, ownership or indebtedness, letters of credit and any documents relating to any rights or obligations thereunder, powers of attorney, goods, wares, merchandise, chattels, stocks on hand, ships, goods on ships, real estate mortgages, deeds of trust, vendors' sales agreements, land contracts, leaseholds, ground rents, real estate and any other interest therein, options, negotiable instruments, trade acceptances, royalties, book accounts, accounts payable, judgments, patents, trademarks or copyrights, insurance policies, safe deposit boxes and their contents, annuities, pooling agreements, services of any nature whatsoever, contracts of any nature whatsoever, and any other property, real, personal, or mixed, tangible or intangible, or interest or interests therein, present, future, or contingent.

§ 542.316 Syria; Syrian.

The term *Syria* means the territory of Syria and any other territory or marine area, including the exclusive economic zone and continental shelf, over which the Government of Syria claims sovereignty, sovereign rights, or jurisdiction, provided that the Government of Syria exercises partial or total de facto control over the area or derives a benefit from economic activity in the area pursuant to an international agreement. The term *Syrian* means pertaining to Syria, as defined in this section.

§ 542.317 Transfer.

The term *transfer* means any actual or purported act or transaction, whether or not evidenced by writing, and whether or not done or performed within the United States, the purpose, intent, or effect of which is to create, surrender, release, convey, transfer, or alter, directly or indirectly, any right, remedy, power, privilege, or interest with respect to any property. Without limitation on the foregoing, it shall include the making, execution, or delivery of any assignment, power, conveyance, check, declaration, deed, deed of trust, power of attorney, power of appointment, bill of sale, mortgage, receipt, agreement, contract, certificate, gift, sale, affidavit, or statement; the making of any payment; the setting off of any obligation or credit; the appointment of any agent, trustee, or fiduciary; the creation or transfer of any lien; the issuance, docketing, filing, or levy of or under any judgment, decree, attachment, injunction, execution, or other judicial or administrative process or order, or the service of any garnishment; the acquisition of any interest of any nature whatsoever by reason of a judgment or decree of any foreign country; the fulfillment of any condition; the exercise of any power of appointment, power of attorney, or other power; or the acquisition, disposition, transportation, importation, exportation, or withdrawal of any security.

§ 542.318   United States.

The term *United States* means the United States, its territories and possessions, and all areas under the jurisdiction or authority thereof.

§ 542.319   United States person; U.S. person.

The term *United States person* or *U.S. person* means any United States citizen, permanent resident alien, entity organized under the laws of the United States or any jurisdiction within the United States (including foreign branches), or any person in the United States.

§ 542.320   U.S. depository institution.

The term *U.S. depository institution* means any entity (including its foreign branches) organized under the laws of the United States or any jurisdiction within the United States, or any agency, office, or branch located in the United States of a foreign entity, that is engaged primarily in the business of banking (for example, banks, savings banks, savings associations, credit unions, trust companies, and United States bank holding companies) and is subject to regulation by federal or state banking authorities.

§ 542.321   U.S. financial institution.

The term *U.S. financial institution* means any U.S. entity (including its foreign branches) that is engaged in the business of accepting deposits, making, granting, transferring, holding, or brokering a loan or other extension of credit, or purchasing or selling foreign exchange, securities, commodity futures or options, or procuring purchasers and sellers thereof, as principal or agent. It includes but is not limited to depository institutions, banks, savings banks, trust companies, securities brokers and dealers, commodity futures and options brokers and dealers, forward contract and foreign exchange merchants, securities and commodities exchanges, clearing corporations, investment companies, employee benefit plans, and U.S. holding companies, U.S. affiliates, or U.S. subsidiaries of any of the foregoing. This term includes those branches, offices, and agencies of foreign financial institutions that are located in the United States, but not such institutions' foreign branches, offices, or agencies.

§ 542.322   U.S. registered broker or dealer in securities.

The term *U.S. registered broker or dealer in securities* means any U.S. citizen, permanent resident alien, or entity organized under the laws of the United States or of any jurisdiction within the United States (including its foreign branches), or any agency, office, or branch of a foreign entity located in the United States, that:

(a) Is a "broker" or "dealer" in securities within the meanings set forth in the Securities Exchange Act of 1934;

(b) Holds or clears customer accounts; and

(c) Is registered with the Securities and Exchange Commission under the Securities Exchange Act of 1934.

§ 542.323   U.S. registered money transmitter.

The term *U.S. registered money transmitter* means any U.S. citizen, permanent resident alien, or entity organized under the laws of the United States or of any jurisdiction within the United States, including its foreign branches, or any agency, office, or branch of a foreign entity located in the United States, that is a money transmitter, as defined in 31 CFR 1010.100(ff)(5), and that is registered pursuant to 31 CFR 1022.380.

Subpart D—Interpretations

§ 542.401   Reference to amended sections.

Except as otherwise specified, reference to any provision in or appendix to this part or chapter or to any regulation, ruling, order, instruction, directive, or license issued pursuant to this part refers to the same as currently amended.

§ 542.402   Effect of amendment.

Unless otherwise specifically provided, any amendment, modification, or revocation of any provision in or appendix to this part or chapter or of any order, regulation, ruling, instruction, or license issued by OFAC does not affect any act done or omitted, or any civil or criminal proceeding commenced or pending, prior to such amendment, modification, or revocation. All penalties, forfeitures, and liabilities under any such order, regulation, ruling, instruction, or license continue and may be enforced as if such amendment, modification, or revocation had not been made.

§ 542.403   Termination and acquisition of an interest in blocked property.

(a) Whenever a transaction licensed or authorized by or pursuant to this part results in the transfer of property (including any property interest) away from the Government of Syria or any other person whose property and interests in property are blocked pursuant to § 542.201(a), such property shall no longer be deemed to be property blocked pursuant to § 542.201(a), unless there exists in the property another interest that is blocked pursuant to § 542.201(a), the transfer of which has not been effected pursuant to license or other authorization.

(b) Unless otherwise specifically provided in a license or authorization issued pursuant to this part, if property (including any property interest) is transferred or attempted to be transferred to the Government of Syria or any other person whose property and interests in property are blocked pursuant to § 542.201(a), such property shall be deemed to be property in which such a person has an interest and therefore blocked.

§ 542.404   Transactions ordinarily incident to a licensed transaction.

(a) Any transaction ordinarily incident to a licensed transaction and necessary to give effect thereto is also authorized, except:

(1) An ordinarily incident transaction, not explicitly authorized within the terms of the license, by or with the Government of Syria or any other person whose property and interests in property are blocked pursuant to § 542.201(a); or

(2) An ordinarily incident transaction, not explicitly authorized within the terms of the license, involving a debit to a blocked account or a transfer of blocked property.

(b) *Example.* A license authorizing a person to complete a securities sale involving Company A, whose property and interests in property are blocked pursuant to § 542.201(a), also authorizes other persons to engage in activities that are ordinarily incident and necessary to complete the sale, including transactions by the buyer, broker, transfer agents, and banks, provided that such other persons are not themselves persons whose property and interests in property are blocked pursuant to § 542.201(a).

§ 542.405   Exportation, reexportation, sale, or supply of services; provision of services.

(a) The prohibition on the exportation, reexportation, sale, or supply of services contained in § 542.207 applies to services performed on behalf of a person in Syria or the Government of Syria or where the benefit of such services is otherwise received in Syria, if such services are performed:

(1) In the United States, or

(2) Outside the United States by a United States person, including by a foreign branch of an entity located in the United States.

(b) The benefit of services performed anywhere in the world on behalf of the Government of Syria is presumed to be received in Syria.

(c) The prohibitions contained in § 542.201 apply to services performed in the United States or by U.S. persons, wherever located, including by a foreign branch of an entity located in the United States:

(1) On behalf of or for the benefit of the Government of Syria or any other person whose property and interests in property are blocked pursuant to § 542.201(a);

(2) With respect to property interests of the Government of Syria or any other person whose property and interests in property are blocked pursuant to § 542.201(a).

(d) *Examples.* (1) U.S. persons may not, except as authorized by or pursuant to this part, provide legal, accounting, financial, brokering, freight forwarding, transportation, public relations, or other services to any person in Syria or to the Government of Syria or any other person whose property and interests in property are blocked pursuant to § 542.201(a).

(2) A U.S. person is engaged in a prohibited exportation of services to Syria when it extends credit to a third-country firm specifically to enable that firm to manufacture goods for sale to Syria or the Government of Syria.

Note to § 542.405: *See* §§ 542.507 and 542.531 on licensing policy with regard to the provision of certain legal and medical services.

§ 542.406 Offshore transactions involving blocked property.

The prohibitions in § 542.201 on transactions or dealings involving blocked property apply to transactions by any U.S. person in a location outside the United States with respect to property held in the name of the Government of Syria or any other person whose property and interests in property are blocked pursuant to § 542.201(a).

§ 542.407 Payments from blocked accounts to satisfy obligations prohibited.

Pursuant to § 542.201, no debits may be made to a blocked account to pay obligations to U.S. persons or other

persons, except as authorized by or pursuant to this part.

Note to § 542.407: *See also* § 542.502(e), which provides that no license or other authorization contained in or issued pursuant to this part authorizes transfers of or payments from blocked property or debits to blocked accounts unless the license or other authorization explicitly authorizes the transfer of or payment from blocked property or the debit to a blocked account.

§ 542.408 Charitable contributions.

Unless specifically authorized by OFAC pursuant to this part, no charitable contribution of funds, goods, services, or technology, including contributions to relieve human suffering, such as food, clothing, or medicine, may be made by, to, or for the benefit of, or received from, the Government of Syria or any other person whose property and interests in property are blocked pursuant to § 542.201(a). For the purposes of this part, a contribution is made by, to, or for the benefit of, or received from, the Government of Syria or any other person whose property and interests in property are blocked pursuant to § 542.201(a) if made by, to, or in the name of, or received from or in the name of, such a person; if made by, to, or in the name of, or received from or in the name of, an entity or individual acting for or on behalf of, or owned or controlled by, such a person; or if made in an attempt to violate, to evade, or to avoid the bar on the provision of contributions by, to, or for the benefit of such a person, or the receipt of contributions from such a person.

§ 542.409 Credit extended and cards issued by U.S. financial institutions.

The prohibition in § 542.201 on dealing in property subject to that section and the prohibition in § 542.207 on exporting services to Syria prohibit U.S. financial institutions from performing under any existing credit agreements, including, but not limited to, charge cards, debit cards, or other credit facilities issued by a U.S. financial institution to the Government of Syria or any other person whose property and interests in property are blocked pursuant to § 542.201(a).

§ 542.410 Setoffs prohibited.

A setoff against blocked property (including a blocked account), whether by a U.S. bank or other U.S. person, is a prohibited transfer under § 542.201 if effected after the effective date.

§ 542.411 Entities owned by a person whose property and interests in property are blocked.

A person whose property and interests in property are blocked pursuant to § 542.201(a) has an interest in all property and interests in property of an entity in which it owns, directly or indirectly, a 50 percent or greater interest. The property and interests in property of such an entity, therefore, are blocked, and such an entity is a person whose property and interests in property are blocked pursuant to § 542.201(a), regardless of whether the entity itself is listed in the Annex to Executive Order 13572, the Annex to Executive Order 13573, or the Annex to Executive Order 13606, or designated pursuant to § 542.201(a).

Note to § 542.411: This section, which deals with the consequences of ownership of entities, in no way limits the definition of the Government of Syria in § 542.305, which includes within its definition other persons whose property and interests in property are blocked but who are not on the SDN list.

§ 542.412 Transactions relating to Syrian petroleum or petroleum products from third countries; transshipments.

(a) Transactions relating to goods containing petroleum or petroleum products of Syrian origin are not prohibited by § 542.208 or § 542.209 if the petroleum or petroleum products have been incorporated into manufactured products or substantially transformed in a third country by a person other than a United States person.

(b) Transactions relating to petroleum or petroleum products of Syrian origin that have not been incorporated into manufactured products or substantially transformed in a third country, including those that have been transshipped through a third country, are prohibited.

§ 542.413 Facilitation; change of policies and procedures; referral of business opportunities offshore.

With respect to § 542.210, a prohibited facilitation or approval of a transaction by a foreign person occurs, among other instances, when a United States person:

(a) Alters its operating policies or procedures, or those of a foreign affiliate, to permit a foreign affiliate to accept or perform a specific contract, engagement or transaction involving Syria or the Government of Syria without the approval of the United States person, where such transaction previously required approval by the United States person and such transaction by the foreign affiliate would be prohibited by this part if performed directly by a United States person or from the United States;

(b) Refers to a foreign person purchase orders, requests for bids, or similar business opportunities involving Syria or the Government of Syria to which the United States person could not directly respond as a result of the prohibitions contained in this part; or

(c) Changes the operating policies and procedures of a particular affiliate with the specific purpose of facilitating transactions that would be prohibited by this part if performed by a United States person or from the United States.

Subpart E—Licenses, Authorizations, and Statements of Licensing Policy

§ 542.501 General and specific licensing procedures.

For provisions relating to licensing procedures, see part 501, subpart E of this chapter. Licensing actions taken pursuant to part 501 of this chapter with respect to the prohibitions contained in this part are considered actions taken pursuant to this part. General licenses and statements of licensing policy relating to this part also may be available through the Syria sanctions page on OFAC's Web site *www.treasury.gov/ofac.*

§ 542.502 Effect of license or authorization.

(a) No license or other authorization contained in this part, or otherwise issued by OFAC, authorizes or validates any transaction effected prior to the issuance of such license or other authorization, unless specifically provided in such license or authorization.

(b) No regulation, ruling, instruction, or license authorizes any transaction prohibited under this part unless the regulation, ruling, instruction, or license is issued by OFAC and specifically refers to this part. No regulation, ruling, instruction, or license referring to this part shall be deemed to authorize any transaction prohibited by any other part of this chapter unless the regulation, ruling, instruction, or license specifically refers to such part.

(c) Any regulation, ruling, instruction, or license authorizing any transaction otherwise prohibited under this part has the effect of removing a prohibition contained in this part from the transaction, but only to the extent specifically stated by its terms. Unless the regulation, ruling, instruction, or license otherwise specifies, such an authorization does not create any right, duty, obligation, claim, or interest in, or with respect to, any property which

would not otherwise exist under ordinary principles of law.

(d) Nothing contained in this part shall be construed to supersede the requirements established under any other provision of law or to relieve a person from any requirement to obtain a license or other authorization from another department or agency of the U.S. Government in compliance with applicable laws and regulations subject to the jurisdiction of that department or agency. For example, exports of goods, services, or technical data which are not prohibited by this part or which do not require a license by OFAC, nevertheless may require authorization by the U.S. Department of Commerce, the U.S. Department of State, or other agencies of the U.S. Government. *See also* § 542.701(f).

(e) No license or other authorization contained in or issued pursuant to this part authorizes transfers of or payments from blocked property or debits to blocked accounts unless the license or other authorization explicitly authorizes the transfer of or payment from blocked property or the debit to a blocked account.

(f) Any payment relating to a transaction authorized in or pursuant to this part that is routed through the U.S. financial system should reference the relevant OFAC general or specific license authorizing the payment to avoid the blocking or rejection of the transfer.

§ 542.503 Exclusion from licenses.

OFAC reserves the right to exclude any person, property, transaction, or class thereof from the operation of any license or from the privileges conferred by any license. OFAC also reserves the right to restrict the applicability of any license to particular persons, property, transactions, or classes thereof. Such actions are binding upon actual or constructive notice of the exclusions or restrictions.

§ 542.504 Payments and transfers to blocked accounts in U.S. financial institutions.

Any payment of funds or transfer of credit in which the Government of Syria or any other person whose property and interests in property are blocked pursuant to § 542.201(a) has any interest that comes within the possession or control of a U.S. financial institution must be blocked in an account on the books of that financial institution. A transfer of funds or credit by a U.S. financial institution between blocked accounts in its branches or offices is authorized, provided that no transfer is made from an account within the

United States to an account held outside the United States, and further provided that a transfer from a blocked account may be made only to another blocked account held in the same name.

Note to § 542.504: *See* § 501.603 of this chapter for mandatory reporting requirements regarding financial transfers. *See also* § 542.203 concerning the obligation to hold blocked funds in interest-bearing accounts.

§ 542.505 Entries in certain accounts for normal service charges authorized.

(a) A U.S. financial institution is authorized to debit any blocked account held at that financial institution in payment or reimbursement for normal service charges owed it by the owner of that blocked account.

(b) As used in this section, the term *normal service charges* shall include charges in payment or reimbursement for interest due; cable, telegraph, Internet, or telephone charges; postage costs; custody fees; small adjustment charges to correct bookkeeping errors; and, but not by way of limitation, minimum balance charges, notary and protest fees, and charges for reference books, photocopies, credit reports, transcripts of statements, registered mail, insurance, stationery and supplies, and other similar items.

Note to § 542.505: *See* § 542.515 which authorizes, subject to certain restrictions, the operation of an account in a U.S. financial institution for an individual in Syria other than an individual whose property and interests in property are blocked pursuant to § 542.201(a).

§ 542.506 Investment and reinvestment of certain funds authorized.

Subject to the requirements of § 542.203, U.S. financial institutions are authorized to invest and reinvest assets blocked pursuant to § 542.201(a), subject to the following conditions:

(a) The assets representing such investments and reinvestments are credited to a blocked account or subaccount that is held in the same name at the same U.S. financial institution, or within the possession or control of a U.S. person, but funds shall not be transferred outside the United States for this purpose;

(b) The proceeds of such investments and reinvestments shall not be credited to a blocked account or subaccount under any name or designation that differs from the name or designation of the specific blocked account or subaccount in which such funds or securities were held; and

(c) No immediate financial or economic benefit accrues (*e.g.,* through pledging or other use) to the

Government of Syria or any other person whose property and interests in property are blocked pursuant to § 542.201(a).

§ 542.507 Provision of certain legal services authorized.

(a) The provision of the following legal services to or on behalf of the Government of Syria or any other person whose property and interests in property are blocked pursuant to § 542.201(a), or to or on behalf of a person in Syria, or in circumstances in which the benefit is otherwise received in Syria is authorized, provided that receipt of payment of professional fees and reimbursement of incurred expenses are authorized by or pursuant to paragraph (d) of this section or otherwise authorized pursuant to this part:

(1) Provision of legal advice and counseling on the requirements of and compliance with the laws of the United States or any jurisdiction within the United States, provided that such advice and counseling are not provided to facilitate transactions in violation of this part;

(2) Representation of persons named as defendants in or otherwise made parties to legal, arbitration, or administrative proceedings before any United States federal, state, or local court or agency;

(3) Initiation and conduct of legal, arbitration, or administrative proceedings before any United States federal, state, or local court or agency;

(4) Representation of persons before any U.S. federal, state, or local court or agency with respect to the imposition, administration, or enforcement of U.S. sanctions against such persons or Syria; and

(5) Provision of legal services in any other context in which prevailing U.S. law requires access to legal counsel at public expense.

(b) The provision of any other legal services to the Government of Syria or any other person whose property and interests in property are blocked pursuant to § 542.201(a), or to or on behalf of a person in Syria, or in circumstances in which the benefit is otherwise received in Syria, not otherwise authorized in this part, requires the issuance of a specific license.

(c) Entry into a settlement agreement or the enforcement of any lien, judgment, arbitral award, decree, or other order through execution, garnishment, or other judicial process purporting to transfer or otherwise alter or affect property or interests in property blocked pursuant to

§ 542.201(a) is prohibited unless licensed pursuant to this part.

(d) *Receipts of payment.* (1) *Legal services to or on behalf of blocked persons.* All receipts of payment of professional fees and reimbursement of incurred expenses for the provision of legal services authorized pursuant to paragraph (a) of this section to or on behalf of the Government of Syria or any other person whose property and interests in property are blocked pursuant to § 542.201(a) must be specifically licensed or otherwise authorized pursuant to § 542.508, which authorizes certain payments from funds originating outside the United States.

(2) *Legal services to or on behalf of all others.* All receipts of payment of professional fees and reimbursement of incurred expenses for the provision of legal services authorized pursuant to paragraph (a) of this section to or on behalf of a person in Syria, or in circumstances in which the benefit is otherwise received in Syria, other than those described in paragraph (d)(1) of this section, are authorized, except that nothing in this section authorizes the debiting of any blocked account or the transfer of any blocked property.

Note to § 542.507: U.S. persons seeking administrative reconsideration or judicial review of their designation or the blocking of their property and interests in property may apply for a specific license from OFAC to authorize the release of a limited amount of blocked funds for the payment of legal fees where alternative funding sources are not available. For more information, see OFAC's *Guidance on the Release of Limited Amounts of Blocked Funds for Payment of Legal Fees and Costs Incurred in Challenging the Blocking of U.S. Persons in Administrative or Civil Proceedings,* which is available on OFAC's Web site at: *www.treasury.gov/ofac.*

§ 542.508 Payments from funds originating outside the United States authorized.

Receipts of payment of professional fees and reimbursement of incurred expenses for the provision of legal services authorized pursuant to § 542.507(a) to or on behalf of the Government of Syria or any other person whose property and interests in property are blocked pursuant to § 542.201(a) are authorized from funds originating outside the United States, provided that:

(a) Prior to receiving payment for legal services authorized pursuant to § 542.507(a) rendered to the Government of Syria or any other person whose property and interests in property are blocked pursuant to § 542.201(a), the U.S. person that is an attorney, law firm, or legal services organization provides to OFAC a copy of a letter of engagement or a letter of

intent to engage specifying the services to be performed and signed by the individual to whom such services are to be provided or, where services are to be provided to an entity, by a legal representative of the entity. The copy of a letter of engagement or a letter of intent to engage, accompanied by correspondence referencing this paragraph (a), is to be mailed to: Licensing Division, Office of Foreign Assets Control, U.S. Department of the Treasury, 1500 Pennsylvania Avenue NW., Annex, Washington, DC 20220;

(b) The funds received by U.S. persons as payment of professional fees and reimbursement of incurred expenses for the provision of legal services authorized pursuant to § 542.507(a) must not originate from:

(1) A source within the United States;

(2) Any source, wherever located, within the possession or control of a U.S. person; or

(3) Any individual or entity, other than the person on whose behalf the legal services authorized pursuant to § 542.507(a) are to be provided, whose property and interests in property are blocked pursuant to any part of this chapter or any Executive order.

Note to paragraph (b) of § 542.508: This paragraph authorizes the blocked person on whose behalf the legal services authorized pursuant to § 542.507(a) are to be provided to make payments for authorized legal services using funds originating outside the United States that were not previously blocked. Nothing in this paragraph authorizes payments for legal services using funds in which any other person whose property and interests in property are blocked pursuant to § 542.201(a), any other part of this chapter, or any Executive order holds an interest.

(c) *Reports.* (1) U.S. persons who receive payments in connection with legal services authorized pursuant to § 542.507(a) must submit quarterly reports no later than 30 days following the end of the calendar quarter during which the payments were received providing information on the funds received. Such reports shall specify:

(i) The individual or entity from whom the funds originated and the amount of funds received; and

(ii) If applicable:

(A) The names of any individuals or entities providing related services to the U.S. person receiving payment in connection with authorized legal services, such as private investigators or expert witnesses;

(B) A general description of the services provided; and

(C) The amount of funds paid in connection with such services.

(2) In the event that no transactions occur or no funds are received during

the reporting period, a statement is to be filed to that effect; and

(3) The reports, which must reference this section, are to be mailed to: Licensing Division, Office of Foreign Assets Control, U.S. Department of the Treasury, 1500 Pennsylvania Avenue NW., Annex, Washington, DC 20220.

Note 1 to § 542.508: U.S. persons who receive payments in connection with legal services authorized pursuant to § 542.507(a) do not need to obtain specific authorization to contract for related services that are ordinarily incident to the provision of those legal services, such as those provided by private investigators or expert witnesses, or to pay for such services. Additionally, U.S. persons do not need to obtain specific authorization to provide related services that are ordinarily incident to the provision of legal services authorized pursuant to § 542.507(a).

Note 2 to § 542.508: Any payment authorized in or pursuant to this paragraph that is routed through the U.S. financial system should reference this § 542.508 to avoid the blocking of the transfer.

Note 3 to § 542.508: Nothing in this section authorizes the transfer of any blocked property, the debiting of any blocked account, the entry of any judgment or order that effects a transfer of blocked property, or the execution of any judgment against property blocked pursuant to any part of this chapter or any Executive order.

§ 542.509 Syrian diplomatic missions in the United States.

(a) The provision of goods or services in the United States to the diplomatic missions of the Government of Syria to the United States and to international organizations in the United States and payment for such goods or services are authorized, provided that:

(1) The goods or services are for the conduct of the official business of the missions, or for personal use of the employees of the missions, and are not for resale;

(2) The transaction does not involve the purchase, sale, financing, or refinancing of real property; and

(3) The transaction is not otherwise prohibited by law.

Note 1 to paragraph (a) of § 542.509: U.S. financial institutions are reminded of their obligation to comply with 31 CFR 501.603.

Note 2 to paragraph (a) of § 542.509: U.S. financial institutions are required to obtain specific licenses to operate accounts for, or extend credit to, the diplomatic missions of the Government of Syria to the United States and to international organizations in the United States.

(b) The provision of goods or services in the United States to the employees of the diplomatic missions of the Government of Syria to the United

States and to international organizations in the United States and payment for such goods or services are authorized, provided that:

(1) The goods or services are for personal use of the employees of the missions, and are not for resale; and

(2) The transaction is not otherwise prohibited by law.

Note to § 542.509: Nothing in this section authorizes the transfer of any property to the Government of Syria, or any other person whose property and interests in property are blocked pursuant to § 542.201(a), other than the diplomatic missions of the Government of Syria to the United States and to international organizations in the United States.

§ 542.510 Exports or reexports to Syria of items licensed or otherwise authorized by the Department of Commerce authorized; exports or reexports of certain services authorized.

(a) The exportation or reexportation of items to Syria from the United States or by a U.S. person, wherever located, to the Government of Syria or any other person whose property and interests in property are blocked pursuant to § 542.201(a), and all transactions ordinarily incident thereto, are authorized, provided that the exportation or reexportation of such items to Syria is licensed or otherwise authorized by the Department of Commerce.

(b) The exportation, reexportation, sale, or supply, directly or indirectly, from the United States or by a U.S. person, wherever located, to Syria, including to the Government of Syria or any other person whose property and interests in property are blocked pursuant to § 542.201(a), of services that are ordinarily incident to the exportation or reexportation of items to Syria, or of services to install, repair, or replace such items, is authorized, provided that the exportation or reexportation of such items to Syria is licensed or otherwise authorized by the Department of Commerce.

(c) This section does not authorize any debit to a blocked account.

Note to § 542.510: This section does not authorize the exportation or reexportation of any item not subject to the Export Administration Regulations, 15 CFR parts 730–774 (the "EAR"), or the exportation or reexportation of services related thereto. *See* 15 CFR 734.3 for a definition of "items subject to the EAR." *See* 31 CFR 542.525 for a general license authorizing the exportation or reexportation of services to Syria related to the exportation or reexportation of certain non-U.S.-origin goods.

§ 542.511 Exportation of certain services incident to Internet-based communications authorized.

(a) To the extent that such transactions are not exempt from the prohibitions of this part, and except as provided in paragraph (b) of this section, the exportation from the United States or by U.S. persons, wherever located, to persons in Syria of services incident to the exchange of personal communications over the Internet, such as instant messaging, chat and email, social networking, sharing of photos and movies, web browsing, and blogging, is authorized, provided that such services are publicly available at no cost to the user.

(b) This section does not authorize:

(1) The direct or indirect exportation of services with knowledge or reason to know that such services are intended for the Government of Syria or any other person whose property and interests in property are blocked pursuant to § 542.201(a);

(2) The direct or indirect exportation of Internet connectivity services or telecommunications transmission facilities (such as satellite or terrestrial network connectivity);

(3) The direct or indirect exportation of web-hosting services that are for purposes other than personal communications (*e.g.,* web-hosting services for commercial endeavors) or of domain name registration services; or

(4) The direct or indirect exportation of any items to Syria.

Note to paragraph (b)(4) of § 542.511: *See* § 542.510 for a general license authorizing the exportation or reexportation of certain items and services to Syria.

(c) Specific licenses may be issued on a case-by-case basis for the exportation of other, including fee-based, services incident to the sharing of information over the Internet.

§ 542.512 Noncommercial, personal remittances authorized.

(a)(1) U.S. persons are authorized to send and receive, and U.S. depository institutions, U.S. registered brokers or dealers in securities, and U.S. registered money transmitters are authorized to process transfers of, funds to or from Syria or for or on behalf of an individual ordinarily resident in Syria in cases in which the transfer involves a noncommercial, personal remittance, provided the transfer is not by, to, or through the Government of Syria or any other person whose property and interests in property are blocked pursuant to § 542.201(a).

(2) Noncommercial, personal remittances do not include charitable donations of funds to or for the benefit

of an entity or funds transfers for use in supporting or operating a business, including a family-owned business.

(b) The transferring institutions identified in paragraph (a) of this section may rely on the originator of a funds transfer with regard to compliance with paragraph (a) of this section, provided that the transferring institution does not know or have reason to know that the funds transfer is not in compliance with paragraph (a) of this section.

(c) An individual who is a U.S. person is authorized to carry funds as a noncommercial, personal remittance, as described in paragraph (a) of this section, to an individual in Syria or ordinarily resident in Syria, other than an individual whose property and interests in property are blocked pursuant to § 542.201(a), provided that the individual who is a U.S. person is carrying the funds on his or her behalf, but not on behalf of another person.

§ 542.513 Official activities of certain international organizations authorized.

(a) Except as provided in paragraphs (b) and (c) of this section, all transactions and activities otherwise prohibited by this part that are for the conduct of the official business of the United Nations, its Specialized Agencies, Programmes, Funds, and Related Organizations by employees, contractors, or grantees thereof are authorized.

Note 1 to paragraph (a) of § 542.513: *See* the United Nations System Organizational Chart at *http://www.un.org/en/aboutun/ structure/pdfs/un-system-chart-color-sm.pdf* for a listing of Specialized Agencies, Programmes, Funds, and Related Organizations of the United Nations.

(b) Contractors or grantees conducting transactions authorized pursuant to paragraph (a) of this section must provide a copy of their contract or grant with the United Nations, or its Specialized Agencies, Programmes, Funds, and Related Organizations to any U.S. person before the U.S. person engages in or facilitates any transaction or activity prohibited by this part. If the contract or grant contains any sensitive or proprietary information, such information may be redacted or removed from the copy given to the U.S. person, provided that the information is not necessary to demonstrate that the transaction is authorized pursuant to paragraph (a) of this section.

(c) This section does not authorize any transactions or activities with or involving persons whose property and interests in property are blocked pursuant to § 542.201(a), other than the Government of Syria.

Note to § 542.513: *See* § 542.510 for a general license authorizing the exportation or reexportation of certain items and services to Syria.

§ 542.514 Transactions related to U.S. persons residing in Syria authorized.

(a) Except as provided in paragraph (b) of this section, individuals who are U.S. persons residing in Syria are authorized to pay their personal living expenses in Syria and to engage in other transactions, including with the Government of Syria, otherwise prohibited by this part that are ordinarily incident and necessary to their personal maintenance within Syria, including, but not limited to, payment of housing expenses, acquisition of goods or services for personal use, payment of taxes or fees to the Government of Syria, and purchase or receipt of permits, licenses, or public utility services from the Government of Syria.

(b) This section does not authorize:

(1) Any debit to a blocked account of the Government of Syria on the books of a U.S. financial institution or to any other account blocked pursuant to § 542.201(a);

(2) Any transaction with a person whose property and interests in property are blocked pursuant to § 542.201(a) other than the Government of Syria; or

(3) Transactions or services ordinarily incident to operating or supporting a business in Syria, employment in Syria, or any new investment in Syria prohibited by § 542.206.

§ 542.515 Operation of accounts authorized.

The operation of an account in a U.S. financial institution for an individual in Syria other than an individual whose property and interests in property are blocked pursuant to § 542.201(a), is authorized, provided that transactions processed through the account:

(a) Are of a personal nature and not for use in supporting or operating a business;

(b) Do not involve transfers directly or indirectly to Syria or for the benefit of individuals ordinarily resident in Syria unless authorized by § 542.512; and

(c) Are not otherwise prohibited by this part.

§ 542.516 Certain services in support of nongovernmental organizations' activities authorized.

(a) Nongovernmental organizations are authorized to export or reexport services to Syria that would otherwise be prohibited by § 542.207 in support of the following not-for-profit activities:

(1) Activities to support humanitarian projects to meet basic human needs in Syria, including, but not limited to, drought relief, assistance to refugees, internally displaced persons, and conflict victims, food and medicine distribution, and the provision of health services;

(2) Activities to support democracy building in Syria, including, but not limited to, rule of law, citizen participation, government accountability, and civil society development projects;

(3) Activities to support education in Syria, including, but not limited to, combating illiteracy, increasing access to education, and assisting education reform projects;

(4) Activities to support non-commercial development projects directly benefiting the Syrian people, including, but not limited to, preventing infectious disease and promoting maternal/child health, sustainable agriculture, and clean water assistance; and

(5) Activities to support the preservation and protection of cultural heritage sites in Syria, including, but not limited to, museums, historic buildings, and archaeological sites.

(b) U.S. depository institutions, U.S. registered brokers or dealers in securities, and U.S. registered money transmitters are authorized to process transfers of funds on behalf of U.S. or third-country non-governmental organizations to or from Syria in support of the activities authorized by paragraph (a), provided that, except as authorized by paragraph (d) of this section, the transfer is not by, to, or through the Government of Syria or any other person whose property and interests in property are blocked pursuant to § 542.201(a).

(c) U.S. persons engaging in transactions pursuant to paragraph (a)(5) or processing transfers of funds to or from Syria in support of activities authorized by paragraph (a)(5) of this section are required to file quarterly reports no later than 30 days following the end of the calendar quarter with OFAC. The reports should include complete information on all activities and transactions undertaken pursuant to paragraph (a)(5) and paragraph (b) in support of the activities authorized by paragraph (a)(5) of this section that took place during the reporting period, including the parties involved, the value of the transactions, the services provided, and the dates of the transactions. The reports should be addressed to the Office of Foreign Assets Control, Licensing Division, U.S. Treasury Department, 1500

Pennsylvania Avenue NW.-Annex, Washington, DC 20220.

(d) Nongovernmental organizations are authorized to engage in transactions with the Government of Syria that are necessary for the activities authorized by paragraph (a) of this section, including, but not limited to, payment of taxes, fees, and import duties to, and purchase or receipt of permits, licenses, or public utility services from, the Government of Syria.

(e) Except as authorized in paragraph (d), this section does not authorize the exportation or reexportation of services to, charitable donations to or for the benefit of, or any other transactions involving, the Government of Syria or any other person whose property and interests in property are blocked pursuant to § 542.201(a). Specific licenses may be issued on a case-by-case basis for these purposes.

Note to § 542.516: *See* § 542.510 for a general license authorizing the exportation or reexportation of certain items and services to Syria.

§ 542.517 Third-country diplomatic and consular funds transfers authorized.

U.S. depository institutions, U.S. registered brokers or dealers in securities, and U.S. registered money transmitters are authorized to process funds transfers for the operating expenses or other official business of third-country diplomatic or consular missions in Syria, provided that the transfer is not by, to, or through the Government of Syria or any other person whose property and interests in property are blocked pursuant to § 542.201(a).

§ 542.518 Payments for overflights of Syrian airspace or emergency landings in Syria authorized.

Payments to Syria of charges for services rendered by the Government of Syria in connection with the overflight of Syria or emergency landing in Syria of aircraft owned or operated by a United States person or registered in the United States are authorized, provided that no payment may be made by, to, or through any person whose property and interests in property are blocked pursuant to § 542.201(a) other than the Government of Syria.

§ 542.519 Transactions related to telecommunications and mail authorized.

(a)(1) Except as provided in paragraph (a)(2) of this section, all transactions with respect to the receipt and transmission of telecommunications involving Syria are authorized, provided that no payment pursuant to this section may involve any debit to a blocked account of the Government of Syria on the books of a U.S. financial institution, or any transaction with a person whose property and interests in property are blocked pursuant to § 542.201(a) other than the Government of Syria.

(2) This section does not authorize:

(i) The provision, sale, or lease of telecommunications equipment or technology; or

(ii) The provision, sale, or lease of capacity on telecommunications transmission facilities (such as satellite or terrestrial network connectivity).

(b) All transactions of common carriers incident to the receipt or transmission of mail and packages between the United States and Syria are authorized, provided that the importation or exportation of such mail and packages is exempt from or authorized pursuant to this part.

§ 542.520 Certain transactions related to patents, trademarks, copyrights, and other intellectual property authorized.

(a) All of the following transactions in connection with patent, trademark, copyright or other intellectual property protection in the United States or Syria are authorized, including exportation of services to Syria, payment for such services, and payment to persons in Syria directly connected to such intellectual property protection:

(1) The filing and prosecution of any application to obtain a patent, trademark, copyright or other form of intellectual property protection;

(2) The receipt of a patent, trademark, copyright, or other form of intellectual property protection;

(3) The renewal or maintenance of a patent, trademark, copyright or other form of intellectual property protection;

(4) The filing and prosecution of opposition or infringement proceedings with respect to a patent, trademark, copyright or other form of intellectual property protection, or the entrance of a defense to any such proceedings; and

(5) The assignment or transfer of a patent, trademark, copyright, or other form of intellectual property protection.

(b) This section authorizes the payment of fees currently due to the United States Government or the Government of Syria, or of the reasonable and customary fees and charges currently due to attorneys or representatives within the United States or Syria, in connection with the transactions authorized in paragraph (a) of this section, except that payment effected pursuant to the terms of this paragraph may not be made from a blocked account.

§ 542.521 Activities and services related to certain nonimmigrant and immigrant categories authorized.

(a) U.S. persons are authorized to engage in all transactions in the United States with persons otherwise eligible for non-immigrant classification under categories A–3 and G–5 (attendants, servants and personal employees of aliens in the United States on diplomatic status), D (crewmen), F (students), I (information media representatives), J (exchange visitors), M (non-academic students), O (aliens with extraordinary ability), P (athletes, artists, and entertainers), Q (international cultural exchange visitors), R (religious workers), or S (witnesses), to the extent such a visa has been granted by the U.S. Department of State or such non-immigrant status, or related benefit, has been granted by the U.S. Department of Homeland Security.

(b) U.S. persons are authorized to engage in all transactions in the United States with persons otherwise eligible for non-immigrant classification under categories E–2 (treaty investor), H (temporary worker), or L (intra-company transferee) and all immigrant classifications, to the extent such a visa has been granted by the U.S. Department of State or such non-immigrant or immigrant status, or related benefit, has been granted by the U.S. Department of Homeland Security, and provided that the persons are not coming to the United States to work as an agent, employee, or contractor of the Government of Syria or an entity in Syria.

(c) U.S. persons are authorized to export services to persons in Syria in connection with the filing of an individual's application for the visa categories listed in paragraphs (a) and (b) of this section.

(d)(1) Accredited U.S. graduate and undergraduate degree-granting academic institutions are authorized to export services to Syria for the filing and processing of applications to enroll, and the acceptance of payments for submitted applications to enroll and tuition from persons ordinarily resident in Syria, provided that any transfer of funds is not by, to, or through the Government of Syria or any other person whose property and interests in property are blocked pursuant to § 542.201(a).

(2) In the event services are exported under paragraph (d)(1) of this section in connection with an application to enroll that is denied or withdrawn, U.S. persons are authorized to transfer, in a lump sum back to Syria or to a third country, any funds paid by the applicant in connection with such an

application, provided that any transfer of funds is not by, to, or through the Government of Syria or any other person whose property and interests in property are blocked pursuant to § 542.201(a).

(e)(1) U.S. persons are authorized to engage in all transactions necessary to export financial services to Syria in connection with an individual's application for a non-immigrant visa under category E–2 (treaty investor) or an immigrant visa under category EB–5 (immigrant investor), provided that any transfer of funds is not by, to, or through the Government of Syria or any other person whose property and interests in property are blocked pursuant to § 542.201(a).

(2) In the event services are exported under paragraph (e)(1) of this section in connection with an application for an E–2 or EB–5 visa that is denied, withdrawn, or otherwise does not result in the issuance of such visa, U.S. persons are authorized to transfer, in a lump sum back to Syria or to a third country, any funds belonging to the applicant that are held in an escrow account during the pendency of, and in connection with such a visa application, provided that any transfer of funds is not by, to, or through the Government of Syria or any other person whose property and interests in property are blocked pursuant to § 542.201(a).

(3) Paragraph (d)(1) of this section does not authorize:

(i) The exportation of financial services by U.S. persons other than in connection with funds used in pursuit of an E–2 or EB–5 visa;

(ii) Any investment in Syria by a U.S. person; or

(iii) The provision of services to any persons coming to the United States to work as an agent, employee, or contractor of the Government of Syria or an entity in Syria.

§ 542.522 Official business of the Federal Government authorized.

(a) All transactions otherwise prohibited by § 542.201(a)(2) that are for the conduct of the official business of the Federal Government by employees, grantees, or contractors thereof, are authorized.

(b) Grantees or contractors conducting transactions authorized pursuant to paragraph (a) of this section must provide a copy of their grant or contract with the United States Government to any U.S. person before the U.S. person engages in or facilitates any transaction prohibited by this part. If the grant or contract contains any sensitive or proprietary information, such information may be redacted or

removed from the copy given to the U.S. person, provided that the information is not necessary to demonstrate that the transaction is authorized pursuant to paragraph (a) of this section.

Note to § 542.522: Section 542.211(d) exempts transactions for the conduct of the official business of the Federal Government by employees, grantees, or contractors thereof to the extent such transactions are subject to the prohibitions contained in this part other than those in § 542.201(a)(2).

§ 542.523 Certain services to the National Coalition of Syrian Revolutionary and Opposition Forces authorized.

(a) Except as provided in paragraphs (b) and (c) of this section, U.S. persons are authorized to export, reexport, sell, or supply, directly or indirectly, to the National Coalition of Syrian Revolutionary and Opposition Forces ("the Coalition") services otherwise prohibited by § 542.207.

Note to paragraph (a): See § 542.510 for a general license authorizing the exportation and reexportation of certain items and services to Syria.

(b) This section does not authorize:

(1) Any transaction with a person whose property and interests in property are blocked pursuant to § 542.201(a); or

(2) The exportation, reexportation, sale, or supply, directly or indirectly, of any services in support of the exportation or reexportation to Syria of any item listed on the United States Munitions List (22 CFR part 121).

(c) Any transfer of funds to or from the Coalition under this section must be conducted through the Coalition's U.S. office through an account of the Coalition at a U.S. financial institution specifically licensed for that purpose by OFAC.

Note to paragraph (c): For additional information on the bank account that is specifically licensed for receipt of funds transfers, please contact the U.S. office of the Coalition at 1101 Pennsylvania Avenue NW., Ste # 6620, Washington, DC 20004, ATTN: OFAC-authorized bank account, or by phone at (202) 800–1130.

Note 1 to § 542.523: Financial institutions transferring funds to or from the Coalition pursuant to this section may rely on the originator of a funds transfer with regard to compliance with paragraph (b), provided that the transferring institution does not know or have reason to know that the funds transfer is not in compliance with paragraph (b) of this section.

Note 2 to § 542.523: Consistent with sections § 542.101 and § 542.502, this section does not authorize any transaction prohibited by any part of 31 CFR Chapter V other than § 542.207. For example, this section does not authorize any transaction with a person

whose property and interests in property are blocked pursuant to § 594.201 of this chapter, such as al-Nusrah.

§ 542.524 Bunkering and emergency repairs.

(a) Except as provided in paragraph (b) of this section, services provided in the United States to a non-Syrian carrier transporting passengers or goods to or from Syria are permissible if they are:

(1) Bunkers or bunkering services;

(2) Supplied or performed in the course of emergency repairs; or

(3) Supplied or performed under circumstances which could not be anticipated prior to the carrier's departure for the United States.

(b) This section does not authorize the provision of services in connection with the transport of any goods to or from the Government of Syria or any other person whose property and interests in property are blocked pursuant to § 542.201(a).

§ 542.525 Exportation or reexportation of services to Syria related to the exportation or reexportation of certain non-U.S.-origin goods authorized.

The exportation, reexportation, sale, or supply, directly or indirectly, from the United States or by a U.S. person, wherever located, to Syria, including to the Government of Syria, of services that are ordinarily incident to the exportation or reexportation to Syria, including to the Government of Syria, of non-U.S.-origin food, medicine, and medical devices that would be designated as EAR 99 under the Export Administration Regulations, 15 CFR parts 730–774 (the "EAR"), if it were subject to the EAR, are authorized.

Note to § 542.525: See § 542.510 for a general license authorizing the exportation or reexportation of certain items and services to Syria from the United States or by a U.S. person.

§ 542.526 Exportation of services related to conferences in the United States or third countries authorized.

(a) The exportation, reexportation, sale, or supply of services from the United States or by a U.S. person are authorized where such services are performed or provided in the United States by or for a person who is ordinarily resident in Syria, other than the Government of Syria or any other person whose property and interests in property are blocked pursuant to § 542.201(a), is authorized, for the purpose of, or which directly relate to, participating in a conference, performance, exhibition or similar event, and such services are consistent with that purpose.

(b) To the extent not otherwise exempt from the prohibitions of this part, the exportation, reexportation, sale, or supply of services directly related to the sponsorship by a U.S. person of a conference or other similar event in a third country that is attended by persons who are ordinarily resident in Syria, other than the Government of Syria or any other person whose property and interests in property are blocked pursuant to § 542.201(a), is authorized, provided that the conference or other similar event is not tailored in whole or in part to or for Syria or persons who are ordinarily resident in Syria.

§ 542.527 Policy on activities related to the telecommunications sector of Syria.

(a) Specific licenses may be issued on a case-by-case basis to authorize U.S. persons to engage in transactions involving Syria's telecommunications sector that are otherwise prohibited by § 542.206, § 542.207, or § 542.210, and that are not otherwise authorized by this part. The purpose of this policy is to enable private persons in Syria to better and more securely access the Internet.

(b) Specific licenses issued pursuant to this policy will not authorize any transaction or activity, directly or indirectly, with the Government of Syria or any other person whose property and interests in property are blocked pursuant to § 542.201(a).

§ 542.528 Policy on activities related to the agricultural sector of Syria.

(a) Specific licenses may be issued on a case-by-case basis to authorize U.S. persons to engage in transactions involving Syria's agricultural sector that are otherwise prohibited by § 542.206, § 542.207, or § 542.210. The purpose of this policy is to enable projects to benefit and support the people of Syria by enhancing and strengthening the agricultural sector in a food insecure country.

(b) Specific licenses issued pursuant to this policy will not authorize any transaction or activity, directly or indirectly, with the Government of Syria or any other person whose property and interests in property are blocked pursuant to § 542.201(a).

§ 542.529 Policy on activities related to petroleum and petroleum products of Syrian origin for the benefit of the National Coalition of Syrian Revolutionary and Opposition Forces.

(a) Specific licenses may be issued on a case-by-case basis to authorize U.S. persons to engage in any transaction otherwise prohibited by § 542.206, § 542.207, § 542.208, § 542.209, or § 542.210, including but not limited to new investment, involving the purchase, trade, export, import, or production of petroleum or petroleum products of Syrian origin for the benefit of the National Coalition of Syrian Revolutionary and Opposition Forces.

(b) Specific licenses issued pursuant to this policy will not authorize any transaction or activity, directly or indirectly, with the Government of Syria or any other person whose property and interests in property are blocked pursuant to § 542.201(a).

§ 542.530 Transactions incident to importations from Syria authorized.

All transactions otherwise prohibited by § 542.207 that are ordinarily incident to an importation into the United States from Syria, directly or indirectly, of goods technology, or services, are authorized, provided the importation is not from or on behalf of, directly or indirectly, a person whose property and interests in property are blocked pursuant to § 542.201(a).

Note to § 542.530: This section does not authorize transactions that are ordinarily incident to an importation that is prohibited pursuant to 542.208 or any transaction prohibited pursuant to 542.209.

§ 542.531 Authorization of emergency medical services.

The provision of nonscheduled emergency medical services in the United States to persons whose property and interests in property are blocked pursuant to § 542.201(a) is authorized, provided that all receipt of payment for such services must be specifically licensed.

Subpart F—Reports

§ 542.601 Records and reports.

For provisions relating to required records and reports, see part 501, subpart C, of this chapter. Recordkeeping and reporting requirements imposed by part 501 of this chapter with respect to the prohibitions contained in this part are considered requirements arising pursuant to this part.

Subpart G—Penalties

§ 542.701 Penalties.

(a) Attention is directed to section 206 of the International Emergency Economic Powers Act (50 U.S.C. 1705) ("IEEPA"), which is applicable to violations of the provisions of any license, ruling, regulation, order, directive, or instruction issued by or pursuant to the direction or authorization of the Secretary of the Treasury pursuant to this part or otherwise under IEEPA.

(1) A civil penalty not to exceed the amount set forth in section 206 of IEEPA may be imposed on any person who violates, attempts to violate, conspires to violate, or causes a violation of any license, order, regulation, or prohibition issued under IEEPA.

Note to paragraph (a)(1) of § 542.701: As of the date of publication in the **Federal Register** of the final rule amending and reissuing this part (May 2, 2014), IEEPA provides for a maximum civil penalty not to exceed the greater of $250,000 or an amount that is twice the amount of the transaction that is the basis of the violation with respect to which the penalty is imposed.

(2) A person who willfully commits, willfully attempts to commit, or willfully conspires to commit, or aids or abets in the commission of a violation of any license, order, regulation, or prohibition may, upon conviction, be fined not more than $1,000,000, or if a natural person, be imprisoned for not more than 20 years, or both.

(b) Attention is directed to section 5 of the United Nations Participation Act, as amended (22 U.S.C. 287c(b)), which provides that any person who willfully violates or evades or attempts to violate or evade any order, rule, or regulation issued by the President pursuant to the authority granted in that section shall, upon conviction, be fined not more than $1,000,000 or, if a natural person, be imprisoned for not more than 20 years, or both.

(c) Violations involving transactions described at section 203(b)(1),(3), and (4) of IEEPA shall be subject only to the penalties set forth in paragraph (b) of this section.

(d) *Adjustments to penalty amounts.* (1) The civil penalties provided in IEEPA are subject to adjustment pursuant to the Federal Civil Penalties Inflation Adjustment Act of 1990 (Pub. L. 101–410, as amended, 28 U.S.C. 2461 note).

(2) The criminal penalties provided in IEEPA and the United Nations Participation Act, as amended (22 U.S.C. 287c) ("UNPA"), are subject to adjustment pursuant to 18 U.S.C. 3571.

(e) Attention is directed to 18 U.S.C. 2332d, which provides that, except as provided in regulations issued by the Secretary of the Treasury, in consultation with the Secretary of State, a U.S. person, knowing or having reasonable cause to know that a country is designated under section 6(j) of the Export Administration Act of 1979, 50 U.S.C. App. 2405, as a country supporting international terrorism, engages in a financial transaction with the government of that country, shall be fined under title 18, United States Code, or imprisoned for not more than 10 years, or both.

(f) Attention is also directed to 18 U.S.C. 1001, which provides that whoever, in any matter within the jurisdiction of the executive, legislative, or judicial branch of the Government of the United States, knowingly and willfully falsifies, conceals, or covers up by any trick, scheme, or device a material fact, or makes any materially false, fictitious, or fraudulent statement or representation, or makes or uses any false writing or document knowing the same to contain any materially false, fictitious, or fraudulent statement or entry shall be fined under title 18, United States Code, or imprisoned, or both.

(g) Violations of this part may also be subject to other applicable laws.

§ 542.702 Pre-Penalty Notice; settlement.

(a) *When required.* If the Office of Foreign Assets Control has reason to believe that there has occurred a violation of any provision of this part or a violation of the provisions of any license, ruling, regulation, order, directive, or instruction issued by or pursuant to the direction or authorization of the Secretary of the Treasury pursuant to this part or otherwise under the International Emergency Economic Powers Act ("IEEPA") and determines that a civil monetary penalty is warranted, the Office of Foreign Assets Control will issue a Pre-Penalty Notice informing the alleged violator of the agency's intent to impose a monetary penalty. A Pre-Penalty Notice shall be in writing. The Pre-Penalty Notice may be issued whether or not another agency has taken any action with respect to the matter. For a description of the contents of a Pre-Penalty Notice, see Appendix A to part 501 of this chapter.

(b)(1) *Right to respond.* An alleged violator has the right to respond to a Pre-Penalty Notice by making a written presentation to the Office of Foreign Assets Control. For a description of the information that should be included in such a response, see Appendix A to part 501 of this chapter.

(2) *Deadline for response.* A response to a Pre-Penalty Notice must be made within the applicable 30-day period set forth in this paragraph. The failure to submit a response within the applicable time period set forth in this paragraph shall be deemed to be a waiver of the right to respond.

(i) *Computation of time for response.* A response to a Pre-Penalty Notice must be postmarked or date-stamped by the U.S. Postal Service (or foreign postal service, if mailed abroad) or courier

service provider (if transmitted to the Office of Foreign Assets Control by courier) on or before the 30th day after the postmark date on the envelope in which the Pre-Penalty Notice was mailed. If the Pre-Penalty Notice was personally delivered by a non-U.S. Postal Service agent authorized by the Office of Foreign Assets Control, a response must be postmarked or date-stamped on or before the 30th day after the date of delivery.

(ii) *Extensions of time for response.* If a due date falls on a federal holiday or weekend, that due date is extended to include the following business day. Any other extensions of time will be granted, at the discretion of the Office of Foreign Assets Control, only upon specific request to the Office of Foreign Assets Control.

(3) *Form and method of response.* A response to a Pre-Penalty Notice need not be in any particular form, but it must be typewritten and signed by the alleged violator or a representative thereof, must contain information sufficient to indicate that it is in response to the Pre-Penalty Notice, and must include the Office of Foreign Assets Control identification number listed on the Pre-Penalty Notice. A copy of the written response may be sent by facsimile, but the original also must be sent to the Office of Foreign Assets Control Enforcement Division by mail or courier and must be postmarked or date-stamped in accordance with paragraph (b)(2) of this section.

(c) *Settlement.* Settlement discussion may be initiated by the Office of Foreign Assets Control, the alleged violator, or the alleged violator's authorized representative. For a description of practices with respect to settlement, see Appendix A to part 501 of this chapter.

(d) *Guidelines.* Guidelines for the imposition or settlement of civil penalties by the Office of Foreign Assets Control are contained in Appendix A to part 501 of this chapter.

(e) *Representation.* A representative of the alleged violator may act on behalf of the alleged violator, but any oral communication with the Office of Foreign Assets Control prior to a written submission regarding the specific allegations contained in the Pre-Penalty Notice must be preceded by a written letter of representation, unless the Pre-Penalty Notice was served upon the alleged violator in care of the representative.

§ 542.703 Penalty imposition.

If, after considering any written response to the Pre-Penalty Notice and any relevant facts, the Office of Foreign Assets Control determines that there

was a violation by the alleged violator named in the Pre-Penalty Notice and that a civil monetary penalty is appropriate, the Office of Foreign Assets Control may issue a Penalty Notice to the violator containing a determination of the violation and the imposition of the monetary penalty. For additional details concerning issuance of a Penalty Notice, see Appendix A to part 501 of this chapter. The issuance of the Penalty Notice shall constitute final agency action. The violator has the right to seek judicial review of that final agency action in federal district court.

§ 542.704 Administrative collection; referral to United States Department of Justice.

In the event that the violator does not pay the penalty imposed pursuant to this part or make payment arrangements acceptable to the Office of Foreign Assets Control, the matter may be referred for administrative collection measures by the Department of the Treasury or to the United States Department of Justice for appropriate action to recover the penalty in a civil suit in a federal district court.

Subpart H—Procedures

§ 542.801 Procedures.

For license application procedures and procedures relating to amendments, modifications, or revocations of licenses; administrative decisions; rulemaking; and requests for documents pursuant to the Freedom of Information and Privacy Acts (5 U.S.C. 552 and 552a), see part 501, subpart E, of this chapter.

§ 542.802 Delegation by the Secretary of the Treasury.

Any action that the Secretary of the Treasury is authorized to take pursuant to E.O. 13338 of May 11, 2004 (69 FR 26751, May 13, 2004) ("E.O. 13338"), E.O. 13399 of April 25, 2006 (71 FR 25059, April 28, 2006), E.O. 13460 of February 13, 2008 (73 FR 8991, February 15, 2008), E.O. 13572 of April 29, 2011 (76 FR 24787, May 3, 2011), E.O. 13573 of May 18, 2011 (76 FR 29143, May 20, 2011), E.O. 13582 of August 17, 2011 (76 FR 52209, August 22, 2011), and E.O. 13606 of April 22, 2012 (77 FR 24571, April 24, 2012), and any further Executive orders relating to the national emergency declared in E.O. 13338, may be taken by the Director of OFAC or by any other person to whom the Secretary of the Treasury has delegated authority so to act.

Subpart I—Paperwork Reduction Act

§ 542.901 Paperwork Reduction Act notice.

For approval by the Office of Management and Budget ("OMB") under the Paperwork Reduction Act of 1995 (44 U.S.C. 3507) of information collections relating to recordkeeping and reporting requirements, licensing procedures (including those pursuant to statements of licensing policy), and other procedures, see § 501.901 of this chapter. An agency may not conduct or sponsor, and a person is not required to respond to, a collection of information unless it displays a valid control number assigned by OMB.

Dated: April 24, 2014.

Adam J. Szubin,
Director, Office of Foreign Assets Control.

Approved: April 24, 2014.

David S. Cohen,
Under Secretary, Office of Terrorism and Financial Intelligence, Department of the Treasury.

[FR Doc. 2014–09998 Filed 5–1–14; 8:45 am]

BILLING CODE 4810–AL–P